The Passion
and
Death of Christ

C. H. Spurgeon

WILLIAM B. EERDMANS PUBLISHING COMPANY
GRAND RAPIDS, MICHIGAN

Reprinted, October 1979

ISBN 0-8028-1187-6

PHOTOLITHOPRINTED BY GRAND RAPIDS BOOK MANUFACTURERS, INC.
GRAND RAPIDS, MICHIGAN

CONTENTS

GETHSEMANE

A Sermon

Text.—"And being in an agony he prayed more earnestly: and his sweat was as it were great drops of blood falling down to the ground."—Luke xxii. 44.

Few had fellowship with the sorrows of Gethsemane. The majority of the disciples were not there. They were not sufficiently advanced in grace to be admitted to behold the mysteries of "the agony." Occupied with the passover feast at their own houses, they represent the many who live upon the letter, but are mere babes and sucklings as to the spirit of the gospel. The walls of Gethsemane fitly typify that weakness in grace which effectually shuts in the deeper marvels of communion from the gaze of ordinary believers. To twelve, nay, to eleven only was the privilege given to enter Gethsemane and see this great sight. Out of the eleven, eight were left at some distance; they had fellowship, but not of that intimate sort to which the men greatly beloved are admitted.

Only three highly favoured ones, who had been with Him on the mount of transfiguration, and had witnessed the life-giving miracle in the house of Jairus—only these three could approach the veil of His mysterious sorrow; within that veil even these must not intrude; a stone's-cast distance must be left between. He must tread the wine-press alone, and of the people there must be none with Him. Peter and the two sons of Zebedee, represent the few eminent, experienced, grace-taught saints, who may be written down as "Fathers"; these having done business on great waters, can in some degree, measure the huge Atlantic waves of their Redeemer's passion; having been much alone with Him, they can read His heart far better than those who merely see Him amid the crowd.

To some selected spirits it is given, for the good of others, and to strengthen them for some future, special, and tremendous conflict, to enter the inner circle and hear the pleadings of the suffering High Priest; they have fellowship with Him in His sufferings, and are made conformable unto His death. Yet I say, even these, the elect out of the elect, these choice and peculiar favourites among the king's courtiers, even these cannot

7

penetrate the secret places of the Saviour's woe, so as to comprehend all His agonies. "Thine unknown sufferings" is the remarkable expression of the Greek liturgy; for there is an inner chamber in His grief, shut out from human knowledge and fellowship. Was it not here that Christ was more than ever an "Unspeakable gift" to us? Is not Watts right when he sings—

> "And all the unknown joys He gives,
> Were bought with agonies unknown."

Since it would not be possible for any believer, however experienced, to know for himself all that our Lord endured in the place of the olive-press, when He was crushed beneath the upper and the nether mill-stone of mental suffering and hellish malice, it is clearly far beyond the preacher's capacity to set it forth to you. Jesus Himself must give you access to the wonders of Gethsemane: as for me, I can but invite you to enter the garden, bidding you put your shoes from off your feet, for the place whereon we stand is holy ground.

Several matters will require our brief consideration. Come Holy Spirit, breathe light into our thoughts, life into our words.

I. Come hither and behold the SAVIOUR'S UNUTTERABLE WOE.

The emotions of that dolorous night are expressed by several words in Scripture. John describes Him as saying four days before His passion, "Now is my soul troubled," as He marked the gathering clouds He hardly knew where to turn Himself, and cried out "What shall I say?" Matthew writes of Him, "he began to be sorrowful and very heavy." Upon the word αδημονειν translated "very heavy," Godwin remarks that there was a distraction in the Saviour's agony since the root of the word signifies "separated from the people—men in distraction, being separated from mankind." What a thought, my brethren, that our blessed Lord should be driven to the very verge of distraction by the intensity of His anguish.

Matthew represents the Saviour Himself as saying "My soul is *exceeding sorrowful*, even unto death." Here the word Περιλυπός means encompassed, encircled, overwhelmed with grief. "He was plunged head and ears in sorrow and had no breathing-hole," is the strong expression of Goodwin. Sin leaves no cranny for comfort to enter, and therefore the sin-bearer must be entirely immersed in woe. Mark records that He began to be *sore amazed*, and to be very heavy. In this case θαμβεισθαι, with the prefix εκ, shews extremity of amazement like that of Moses when he did exceedingly fear and quake. O blessed Saviour, how can we bear to think of Thee as a Man astonished and alarmed! Yet was it even so when the terrors of God set themselves in array against Thee.

Luke uses the strong language of my text—"being in an agony." These expressions, each of them worthy to be the theme of a discourse, are quite sufficient to show that the grief of the Saviour was of the most extraordinary character; well justifying the prophetic exclamation, "Behold and see if there be any sorrow like unto my sorrow which was done unto me." He stands before us peerless in misery. None are molested by the powers of evil as He was; as if the powers of hell had given commandment to their legions, "Fight neither with small nor great, save only with the king himself."

Should we profess to understand all the sources of our Lord's agony, wisdom would rebuke us with the question "Hast thou entered into the springs of the sea? or hast thou walked in search of the depths?" We cannot do more than look at the revealed causes of grief. It partly arose from the horror of His soul *when fully comprehending the meaning of sin.* Brethren, when you were first convinced of sin and saw it as a thing exceeding sinful, though your perception of its sinfulness was but faint compared with its real heinousness, yet horror took hold upon you. Do you remember those sleepless nights? Like the Psalmist, you said "My bones waxed old through my roaring all the day long, for day and night thy hand was heavy upon me; my moisture is turned into the drought of summer."

Some of us can remember when our souls chose strangling rather than life; when if the shadows of death could have covered us from the wrath of God we would have been too glad to sleep in the grave that we might not make our bed in hell. Our blessed Lord saw sin in its natural blackness. He had a most distinct perception of its treasonable assault upon His God, its murderous hatred to Himself, and its destructive influence upon mankind. Well might horror take hold upon Him, for a sight of sin must be far more hideous than a sight of hell, which is but its offspring.

Another deep fountain of grief was found in the fact that Christ now *assumed more fully His official position with regard to sin.* He was now made *sin.* Hear the word! He, Who knew no sin, was made *sin* for us, that we might be made the righteousness of God in Him. In that night the words of Isaiah were fulfilled— "The Lord hath laid on him the iniquity of us all." Now He stood as the sin-bearer, the substitute accepted by Divine justice to bear that we might never bear the whole of wrath divine. At that hour heaven looked on Him as standing in the sinner's stead, and treated as sinful man had richly deserved to be treated. Oh! dear friends, when the immaculate Lamb of God found Himself in the place of the guilty, when He could not repudiate that place because He had voluntarily accepted it in order to save His chosen, what must His soul have felt, how must His perfect nature have been shocked at such close association with iniquity?

We believe that at this time, *our Lord had a very clear view of all the shame and suffering of His crucifixion.* The agony was but one of the first drops of the tremendous shower which discharged itself upon His head. He foresaw the speedy coming of the traitor-disciple, the seizure by the officers, the mock-trials before the Sanhedrim, and Pilate, and Herod, the scourging and buffeting, the crown of thorns, the shame, the spitting. All these rose up before His mind, and, as it is a general law of our nature that the foresight of trial is more grievous than trial itself, we can conceive how it was that He Who answered not a word when in the midst of the conflict, could not restrain Himself from strong crying and tears in the prospect of it. Beloved friends, if you can revive before your mind's eye the terrible incidents of His death, the hounding through the streets of Jerusalem, the nailing to the cross, the fever, the thirst, and, above all, the forsaking of His God, you cannot marvel that He began to be very heavy, and was sore amazed.

But possibly a yet more fruitful tree of bitterness was this—*that now His Father began to withdraw His presence from Him.* The shadow of that great eclipse began to fall upon His spirit when He knelt in that cold midnight amidst the olives of Gethsemane. The sensible comforts which had cheered His spirit were taken away; that blessed application of promises which Christ Jesus needed as a man, was removed; all that we understand by the term "consolations of God" were hidden from His eyes. He was left single-handed in His weakness to contend for the deliverance of man. The Lord stood by as if He were an indifferent spectator, or rather, as if He were an adversary, He wounded Him "with the wound of an enemy, with the chastisement of a cruel one."

But in our judgment the fiercest heat of the Saviour's suffering in the garden lay in *the temptations of Satan.* That hour above any time in His life, even beyond the forty days' conflict in the wilderness, was *the time of His temptation.* "This is your hour and the power of darkness." Now could *He* emphatically say, "The prince of this world cometh." This was His last hand-to-hand fight with all the hosts of hell, and here must He sweat great drops of blood before the victory can be achieved.

II. Turn we next to contemplate THE TEMPTATION OF OUR LORD.

At the outset of His career, the serpent began to nibble at the heel of the promised deliverer; and now as the time approached when the seed of the woman should bruise the serpent's head, that old dragon made a desperate attempt upon his great destroyer. It is not possible for us to lift the veil where revelation has permitted it to fall, but we can form some faint idea of the suggestions with which Satan tempted our Lord. Let us, however, remark by way of caution, before we attempt to paint this picture, that whatever Satan may have suggested to our Lord, His perfect nature did not in any degree whatever submit to it so as to sin. The temptations were, doubtless, of the very foulest character, but they left no speck or flaw upon Him, Who remained still the fairest among ten thousand. The prince of this world came, but He had nothing in Christ. He struck the sparks, but they did not fall, as in our case, upon dry tinder; they fell as into the sea, and were quenched at once. He hurled the fiery arrows, but they could not even scar the flesh of Christ; they smote upon the buckler of His perfectly righteous nature, and they fell off with their points broken, to the discomfiture of the adversary.

But what, think you, were these temptations? It strikes me, from some hints given, that they were somewhat as follows— there was, first, *a temptation to leave the work unfinished;* we may gather this from the prayer—"If it be possible, let this cup pass from me." "Son of God," the tempter said, "is it so? Art Thou really called to bear the sin of man? Hath God said, 'I have laid help upon one that is mighty,' and art thou He, the chosen of God, to bear all this load? Look at thy weakness! Thou sweatest, even now, great drops of blood; surely thou art not He Whom the father hath ordained to be mighty to save; or if Thou be, what wilt Thou win by it? What will it avail Thee? Thou hast glory enough already. See what miscreants they are for whom Thou art to offer up Thyself a sacrifice. Thy best friends are asleep about Thee when most Thou needest their comfort; Thy treasurer, Judas, is hastening to betray Thee for the price of a common slave. The world for which Thou sacrificest Thyself will cast out Thy name as evil, and Thy Church, for which Thou dost pay the ransom-price, what is it worth? A company of mortals! Thy divinity could create the like any moment it pleaseth Thee; why needest Thou, then, pour out Thy soul unto death?" Such arguments would Satan use; the hellish craft of one who had then been thousands of years tempting men, would know how to invent all manner of mischief. He would pour the hottest coals of hell upon the Saviour. It was in struggling with this temptation, among others, that, being in an agony, our Saviour prayed more earnestly.

Scripture implies that our Lord was assailed by *the fear that His strength would not be sufficient.* He was heard in that He feared. How, then, was He heard? An angel was sent unto Him strengthening Him. His fear, then, was probably produced by a sense of weakness. I imagine that the foul fiend would whisper in His ear—"Thou! Thou endure to be smitten of God and abhorred of men! Reproach hath broken Thy heart already; how wilt Thou bear to be publicly put to shame and driven without the city as an unclean thing? How wilt Thou bear to see Thy weeping kinsfolk and Thy broken-hearted mother standing at the foot of Thy cross? Thy tender and sensitive spirit will quail under it. As for Thy body, it is already emaciated; Thy long fastings have brought Thee very low; Thou wilt become a prey to death long ere Thy work is done. Thou wilt surely fail. God hath forsaken Thee. Now will they persecute and take Thee; they will give up Thy soul to the lion, and Thy darling to the power of the dog."

Then would he picture all the sufferings of crucifixion, and say, "Can thine heart endure, or can thine hands be strong in the day when the Lord shall deal with Thee?" The temptation of Satan was not directed against the Godhead, but the manhood of Christ, and therefore the fiend would probably dwell upon the feebleness of man. "Didst Thou not say Thyself, 'I am a worm and no man, the reproach of men and the despised of the people?' How wilt Thou bear it when the wrathclouds of God gather about Thee? The tempest will surely shipwreck all Thy hopes. It cannot be; Thou canst not drink of this cup, nor be baptized with this baptism."

In this manner, we think, was our Master tried. But see He yields not to it. Being in an agony, which word means in a wrestling, He struggles with the tempter like Jacob with the angel. "Nay," saith He, "I will not be subdued by taunts of My weakness; I am strong in the strength of My Godhead, I will overcome thee yet." Yet was the temptation so awful, that, in order to master it, His mental depression caused Him to "sweat as it were great drops of blood falling down to the ground."

Possibly, also, the temptation may have arisen from a suggestion *that He was utterly forsaken.* I do not know—there may be sterner trials than this, but surely this is *one* of the worst, to be utterly forsaken. "See," said Satan, as he hissed it out between his teeth—"see, Thou hast a friend nowhere! Look up to heaven, Thy Father hath shut up the bowels of His compassion against Thee. Not an angel in Thy Father's courts will stretch out his hand to help Thee. Look Thou yonder, not one of those spirits who honoured Thy birth will interfere to protect Thy life. All heaven is false to Thee; Thou art left alone. And as for earth, do not all men thirst for Thy blood? Lo! Thou hast no friend left in heaven or earth. All hell is against Thee. I have stirred up mine infernal den. I have sent my missives throughout all regions summoning every prince of darkness to set upon Thee this night, and we will spare no arrows, we will use all our infernal might to overwhelm Thee; and what wilt Thou do, Thou solitary one?" It may be, this was the temptation; I think it was, because the appearance of an angel unto Him strengthening Him removed that fear. He was heard in that He feared; He was no more alone, but heaven was with Him.

We think Satan also assaulted our Lord with a bitter taunt indeed. You know in what guise the tempter can dress it, and how bitterly sarcastic he can make the insinuation—"Ah! *Thou wilt not be able to achieve the redemption of Thy people.* Thy grand benevolence will prove a mockery, and Thy beloved ones will perish. Thou shalt not prevail to save them from my grasp. Thy scattered sheep shall surely be my prey. Son of David, I am a match for Thee; Thou canst not deliver out of my hand. Many of Thy chosen have entered heaven on the strength of Thine atonement, but I will drag them thence, and quench the stars of glory; I will thin the courts of heaven of the choristers of God, for Thou wilt not fulfil Thy suretyship; Thou canst not do it. Thou art not able to bring up all this great people; they will perish yet. See, are not the sheep scattered now that the Shepherd is smitten? They will all forget Thee. Thou wilt never see of the travail of Thy soul. Thy desired end will never be reached. Thou wilt be for ever the man that began to build but was not able to finish."

Perhaps this is more truly the reason why Christ went three times to look at His disciples. You have seen a mother; she is very faint, weary with a heavy sickness, but she labours under a sore dread that her child will die. She has started from her couch, upon which disease had thrown her, to snatch a moment's rest. She gazes anxiously upon her child. She marks the faintest sign of recovery. But she is sore sick herself, and cannot remain more than an instant from her own bed. She cannot sleep, she tosses painfully, for her thoughts wander; she rises to gaze again —"How art thou, my child, how art thou? Are those palpitations of thy heart less violent? Is thy pulse more gentle?" But, alas! she is faint, and she must go to her bed again, yet she can get no rest. She will return again and again to watch the loved one. So, methinks, Christ looked upon Peter, and James, and John, as much as to say, "No, they are not all lost yet; there are three left"; and, looking upon them as the type of all the Church, He seemed to say—"No, no; I will overcome; I will get the mastery; I will struggle even unto blood; I will pay the ransom-price, and deliver My darlings from their foe."

Now these, methinks, were His temptations. If you can form a fuller idea of what they were than this, then right happy shall

B

I be. With this one lesson I leave the point—"*Pray that ye enter not into temptation.*" This is Christ's own expression; His own deduction from His trial. You have all read, dear friends, John Bunyan's picture of Christian fighting with Apollyon. That master-painter has sketched it to the very life. He says, though "this sore combat lasted for above half a day, even till Christian was almost quite spent, I never saw him all the while give so much as one pleasant look, till he perceived he had wounded Apollyon with his two-edged sword; then, indeed, he did smile and look upward! But it was the dreadfullest sight I ever saw." That is the meaning of that prayer, "Lead us not into temptation."

Oh you that go recklessly where you are tempted, you that pray for afflictions—and I have known some silly enough to do that—you that put yourselves where you tempt the devil to tempt you, take heed from the Master's own example. He sweats great drops of blood when He is tempted. Oh! pray God to spare you such a trial. Pray this morning and every day, "Lead me not into temptation."

III. Behold, dear brethren, THE BLOODY SWEAT.

We read, that "he sweats as it were great drops of blood." This phenomenon, though somewhat unusual, has been witnessed in other persons. There are several cases on record, some in the old medicine books of Galen, and others of more recent date, of persons who after long weakness, under fear of death have sweat blood. But this case is altogether one by itself for several reasons. If you will notice, He not only sweat blood, but it was in great drops; the blood coagulated, and formed large masses. I cannot better express what is meant than by the word "gouts"—big, heavy drops. This has not been seen in any case. Some slight effusions of blood have been known in cases of persons who were previously enfeebled, but great drops never. Here He stands unrivalled. He was a man in good health, only about thirty years of age, and was labouring under no fear of death; but the mental pressure arising from His struggle with temptation, and the straining of all His strength, in order to baffle the temptation of Satan, so forced His frame to an unnatural excitement, that His pores sent forth great drops of blood which fell down to the ground. This proves how tremendous must have been the weight of sin when it was able so to crush the Saviour that He distilled drops of blood! This proves too, my brethren, the mighty power of His love.

It is a very pretty observation of old Isaac Ambrose that the gum which exudes from the tree without cutting is always the best. This precious, camphire-tree yielded most sweet spices when it was wounded under the knotty whips and when it was pierced by the nails on the cross; but see, it giveth forth its best spice when there is no whip, no nail, no wound. This sets forth the voluntariness of Christ's sufferings, since without a lance the blood flowed freely. No need to put on the leech, or apply the knife; it flows spontaneously. No need for the rulers to cry "Spring up, O well"; of itself it flows in crimson torrents.

Dearly beloved friends, if men suffer some frightful pain of mind—I am not acquainted with the medical matter—apparently the blood rushes to the heart. The cheeks are pale; a fainting fit comes on; the blood has gone inward, as if to nourish the inner man while passing through its trial. But see our Saviour in His agony; He is so utterly oblivious of self, that instead of His agony driving His blood to the heart to nourish himself, it drives it outward to bedew the earth. The agony of Christ, inasmuch as it pours Him out upon the ground, pictures the fulness of the offering which He made for men.

Do you not perceive, my brethren, how intense must have been the wrestling through which He passed, and will you not hear its voice *to you?*—"Ye have not yet resisted unto blood, striving against sin." It has been the lot of some of us to have sore temptations—else we did not know how to teach others—so sore that in wrestling against them the cold, clammy sweat has stood upon our brow. The place will never be forgotten by me—a lonely spot; where, musing upon my God, an awful rush of blasphemy went over my soul, till I would have preferred death to the trial; and I fell on my knees there and then, for the agony was awful, while my hand was at my mouth to keep the blasphemies from being spoken.

Once let Satan be permitted really to try you with a temptation to blasphemy, and you will never forget it, though you live till your hairs are blanched; or let him attack you with some lust, and though you hate and loathe the very thought of it, and would lose your right arm sooner than indulge in it, yet it will come, and hunt, and persecute, and torment you. Wrestle against it even unto sweat, my brethren, yea, even unto blood. Pray that ye enter not into temptation, so that when ye enter into it ye may with confidence say, "Lord, I did not seek this, therefore help me through with it, for Thy name's sake."

IV. I want you, in the fourth place, to notice THE SAVIOUR'S PRAYER.

Dear friends, when we are tempted and desire to overcome, the best weapon is prayer. When you cannot use the sword and the shield, take to yourself the famous weapon of All-prayer. So your Saviour did. Let us notice His prayer. *It was lonely prayer.* He withdrew even from His three best friends about a stone's cast. Believer, especially in temptation, be much in solitary prayer. As private prayer is the key to open heaven, so is it the key to shut the gates of hell. As it is a shield to prevent, so is it the sword with which to fight against temptation. Family-prayer, social prayer, prayer in the Church, will not suffice, these are very precious, but the best beaten spice will smoke in your censer in your private devotions, where no ear hears but God. Betake yourselves to solitude if you would overcome.

Mark, too, it was *humble prayer*. Luke says He knelt, but another evangelist says He fell on His face. What! does the King fall on His face? Where, then, must be thy place, thou humble servant of the great Master? Doth the Prince fall flat to the ground? Where, then, wilt thou lie? What dust and ashes shall cover thy head? What sackcloth shall gird thy loins? Humility gives us good foot-hold in prayer. There is no hope of any real prevalence with God, who casteth down the proud, unless we abase ourselves that He may exalt us in due time.

Further, it was *filial prayer*. Matthew describes Him as saying "O my Father," and Mark puts it, "Abba, Father." You will find this always a stronghold in the day of trial to plead your adoption. Hence that prayer, in which it is written, "Lead us not into temptation, but deliver us from evil," begins with "Our Father which art in heaven." Plead as a child. You have no rights as a subject; you have forfeited them by your treason, but nothing can forfeit a child's right to a father's protection. Be not then ashamed to say, "My Father, hear my cry."

Again, observe that it was *persevering prayer*. He prayed three times, using the same words. Be not content until you prevail. Be as the importunate widow, whose continual coming earned what her first supplication could not win. Continue in prayer, and watch in the same with thanksgiving.

Further, see how it glowed to a red-hot heat—*it was earnest prayer*. "He prayed more earnestly." What groans were those which were uttered by Christ! What tears, which welled up from the deep fountains of His nature! Make earnest supplication if you would prevail against the adversary.

And last, *it was the prayer of resignation*. "Nevertheless, not as I will, but as thou wilt." Yield, and God yields. Let it be as God wills, and God will will it that it shall be for the best. Be thou perfectly content to leave the result of thy prayer in His hands, Who knows when to give, and how to give, and what to give, and what to withhold. So pleading, earnestly, importunately, yet mingling with it humility and resignation, thou shalt yet prevail.

Dear friends, we must conclude, turn to the last point with this as a practical lesson—"*Rise and pray*." When the disciples were lying down they slept; sitting was the posture that was congenial to sleep. Rise; shape yourselves; stand up in the name of God; rise and pray. And if you are in temptation, be you more than ever you were in your life before, instant, passionate, importunate with God that He should deliver you in the day of your conflict.

V. As time has failed us we close with the last point, which is, THE SAVIOUR'S PREVALENCE.

The cloud has passed away. Christ has knelt, and the prayer is over. "But," says one, "did Christ prevail in prayer?" Beloved, could we have any hope that He would prevail in heaven if He had not prevailed on earth? Should we not have had a suspicion that if His strong crying and tears had not been heard *then*, He would fail *now?* His prayers did speed, and therefore He is a good intercessor for us. "How was He heard?" The answer shall be given very briefly indeed. He was heard, I think, in three respects. The first gracious answer that was given Him was, *that His mind was suddenly rendered calm.* What a difference there is between "My soul is exceeding sorrowful,"— His hurrying to and fro, His repetition of the prayer three times, the singular agitation that was upon Him—what a contrast between all these and His going forth to meet the traitor with "Betrayest thou the Son of Man with a kiss?" Like a troubled sea before, and now as calm as when He Himself said, "Peace be still," and the waves were quiet.

You cannot know a profounder peace than that which reigned in the Saviour when before Pilate He answered him not a word. He is calm to the last, as calm as though it were His day of triumph rather than His day of trouble. Now I think this was vouchsafed to Him in answer to His prayer. He had sufferings perhaps more intense, but His mind was now quieted so as to meet them with greater deliberation.

Next, we believe that He was answered *by God strengthening Him through an angel.* How that was done we do not know. Probably it was by what the angel said, and equally likely is it that it was by what he did. The angel may have whispered the promises; pictured before His mind's eye the glory of His success; sketched His resurrection; portrayed the scene when His angels would bring His chariots from on high to bear Him to His throne; revived before Him the recollection of the time of His advent, the prospect when He should reign from sea to sea, and from the river even to the ends of the earth; and so have made Him strong. Or, perhaps, by some unknown method God sent such power to our Christ, who had been like Samson with his locks shorn, that He suddenly received all the might and majestic energy that were needed for the terrific struggle. Then He walked out of the garden no more a worm and no man, but made strong with an invisible might that made Him a match for all the armies that were round about Him.

And I think we may conclude with saying, that God heard Him in granting Him now, not simply strength, *but a real victory over Satan.* I do not know whether what Adam Clarke supposes is correct, that in the garden Christ did pay more of the price than he did even on the cross; but I am quite convinced that they are very foolish who get to such refinement that they think the atonement was made on the cross, and nowhere else at all. We believe that it was made in the garden as well as on the cross; and it strikes me that in the garden one part of Christ's work was finished, wholly finished and that was His conflict with Satan. I conceive that Christ had now rather to bear the absence of His Father's presence and the revilings of the people and the sons of men, than the temptations of the devil. I do think that these were over when He rose from His knees in prayer, when He lifted Himself from the ground where He marked His visage in the clay in drops of blood. The temptation of Satan was then over, and He might have said concerning that part of the work—"It is finished; broken is the dragon's head; I have overcome him." If this be so, Christ was then heard in that He feared; He feared the temptation of Satan, and He was delivered from it; He feared His own weakness, and He was strengthened; He feared His own trepidation of mind, and He was made calm.

What shall we say, then, in conclusion, but this lesson. Does it not say "Whatsoever ye shall ask in prayer, believing, ye shall have." Then if your temptations reach the most tremendous height and force, still lay hold of God in prayer and you shall prevail. Convinced sinner! that is a comfort for you. Troubled saint! that is a joy for you. To one and all of us is this lesson of this morning—"Pray that ye enter not into temptation." If in temptation let us ask that Christ may pray for us that our faith fail not, and when we have passed through the trouble let us try to strengthen our brethren, even as Christ has strengthened us this day.

BARABBAS PREFERRED TO JESUS

A SERMON

Text.—"Then cried they all again, saying, Not this man, but Barabbas. Now Barabbas was a robber."—John xviii. 40.

THE custom of delivering a prisoner upon the day of the passover was intended no doubt as an act of grace on the part of the Roman authorities towards the Jews, and by the Jews it may have been accepted as a significant compliment to their passover. Since on that day they themselves were delivered out of the land of Egypt, they may have thought it to be most fitting that some imprisoned person should obtain his liberty. There was no warrant however in Scripture for this, it was never commanded by God, and it must have had a very injurious effect upon public justice, that the ruling authority should discharge a criminal, some one quite irrespective of his crimes or of his repentance; letting him loose upon society, simply and only because a certain day must be celebrated in a peculiar manner.

Since some one prisoner must be delivered on the paschal day, Pilate thinks that he has now an opportunity of allowing the Saviour to escape without at all compromising his character with the authorities at Rome. He asks the people which of the two they will prefer, a notorious thief then in custody, or the Saviour. It is probable that Barabbas had been, till that moment, obnoxious to the crowd; and yet, notwithstanding his former unpopularity—the multitude, instigated by the priests, forget all his faults, and prefer him to the Saviour.

Who Barabbas was, we cannot exactly tell. His name, as you in a moment will understand, even if you have not the slightest acquaintance with Hebrew, signifies "his father's son," "*Bar*" signifying "son," as when Peter is called Simon Bar-jonas, son of Jonas; the other part of his name "*Abbas*," signifying "father"—"abbas" being the word which we use in our filial aspirations, "Abba Father." Barabbas, then, is the "son of his father"; and some mystics think that there is an imputation here, that he was particularly and specially a son of Satan.

Others conjecture that it was an endearing name, and was given him because he was his father's darling, an indulged child; his father's boy, as we say; and these writers add that indulged children often turn out to be imitators of Barabbas, and are the most likely persons to become injurious to their country, griefs to their parents, and curses to all about them. If it be so, taken in connection with the case of Absalom, and especially of Eli's sons, it is a warning to parents that they err not in excessive indulgence of their children. Barabbas appears to have committed three crimes at the least: he was imprisoned for murder, for sedition, and for felony—a sorry combination of offences, certainly; we may well pity the sire of such a son.

This wretch is brought out and set in competition with Christ. The multitude are appealed to. Pilate thinks that from the sense of shame they really cannot possibly prefer Barabbas; but they are also so blood-thirsty against the Saviour, and are so moved by the priests, that with one consent—there does not appear to have been a single objecting voice, nor one hand held up to the contrary—with a marvellous unanimity of voice, they cry, "Not this man, but Barabbas," though they must have known, since he was a *notable* well-known offender, that Barabbas was a murderer, a felon, and a traitor.

This fact is very significant. There is more teaching in it than at first sight we might imagine. Have we not here, first of all, in this act of the deliverance of the sinner and the binding of the innocent, a sort of type of that great work which is accomplished by the death of our Saviour? You and I may fairly take our stand by the side of Barabbas. We have robbed God of His glory; we have been seditious traitors against the government of heaven: if he who hateth his brother be a murderer, we also have been guilty of that sin. Here we stand before the judgment-seat; the Prince of Life is bound for us and we are suffered to go free. The Lord delivers us and acquits us, while the Saviour, without spot or blemish, or shadow of a fault, is led forth to crucifixion.

Two birds were taken in the rite of the cleansing of a leper. The one bird was killed, and its blood was poured into a basin; the other bird was dipped in this blood, and then, with its wings all crimson, it was set free to fly into the open field. The bird slain well pictures the Saviour, and every soul that has by faith been dipped in His blood, flies upward towards heaven singing sweetly in joyous liberty, owing life and liberty entirely to Him who was slain. It comes to this, Barabbas must die or Christ must die; you the sinner must perish, or Christ Immanuel, the Immaculate, must die. He dies that we may be delivered. Oh! have we all a participation in such a deliverance to-day? and though we have been robbers, traitors, and murderers yet we can rejoice that Christ has delivered us from the curse of the law, having been made a curse for us?

The transaction has yet another voice. This episode in the Saviour's history shows that in the judgment of the people, Jesus Christ was a greater offender than Barabbas; and, for once, I may venture to say, that *vox populi* (the voice of the people), which in itself was a most infamous injustice, if it be read in the light of the imputation of our sins to Christ, was *vox Dei* (the voice of God). Christ, as He stood covered with His people's sins, had more sin laid upon Him than that which rested upon Barabbas. In Him was no sin; He was altogether incapable of becoming a sinner: holy, harmless, and undefiled is Christ Jesus, but He takes the whole load of His people's guilt upon Himself by imputation, and as Jehovah looks upon Him, He sees more guilt lying upon the Saviour, than even upon this atrocious sinner, Barabbas. Barabbas goes free—innocent—in comparison with the tremendous weight which rests upon the Saviour. Think, beloved, then, how low your Lord and Master stooped to be thus *numbered with the transgressors.* Watts has put it strongly, but, I think, none too strongly—

> "His honour and His breath
> Were taken both away,
> Join'd with the wicked in His death,
> And made as vile as they."

He was so in the estimation of the people, and before the bar of justice, for the sins of the whole company of the faithful were made to meet upon Him. "The Lord hath laid upon him the iniquity of us all." What that iniquity must have been, no heart can conceive, much less can any tongue tell. Measure it by the griefs He bore, and then, if you can guess what these were, you can form some idea of what must have been the guilt which sunk Him lower before the bar of justice than even Barabbas himself. Oh! what condescension is here! The just One dies for the unjust. He bears the sin of many, and makes intercession for the transgressors.

Yet, again, there seems to me to be a third lesson, before I come to that which I want to enforce from the text. Our Saviour knew that His disciples would in all ages be hated by the world far more than outward sinners. Full often the world has been more willing to put up with murderers, thieves, and drunkards, than with Christians; and it has fallen to the lot of some of the best and most holy of men to be so slandered and abused that their names have been cast out as evil, scarcely worthy to be written in the same list with criminals. Now, Christ has sanctified these sufferings of His people from the slander of their enemies, by bearing just such sufferings Himself, so that, my brethren, if you or I should find ourselves charged with crimes which we abhor, if our heart should be ready to burst under the accumulation of slanderous venom, let us lift up our head and feel that in all this we have a Comrade who has true fellowship with us, even the Lord Jesus Christ, who was rejected when Barabbas was selected. Expect no better treatment than your master. Remember that the disciple is not above his Lord. If they have called the Master of the house Beelzebub, much more will they call them of His household; and if they prefer the murderer to Christ, the day may not be distant when they will prefer even a murderer to you.

These things seem to me to lie upon the surface; I now come to our more immediate subject. First, we shall consider *the sin as it stands in the Evangelical history;* second, we shall observe that *this is the sin of the whole world;* thirdly, that *this sin we ourselves were guilty of before conversion;* and fourthly, that *this is, we fear, the sin of very many persons who are here this morning:* we shall talk with them and expostulate, praying that the Spirit of God may change their hearts and lead them to accept the Saviour.

I. A few minutes may be profitably spent in CONSIDERING, THEN, THE SIN AS WE FIND IT IN THIS HISTORY.

They preferred Barabbas to Christ. The sin will be more clearly seen if we remember that *the Saviour had done no ill.* No law, either of God or man, had He broken. He might truly have used the words of Samuel—"Behold, here I am: witness against me before the Lord, and before his anointed; whose ox have I taken? or whose ass have I taken? or whom have I defrauded? whom have I oppressed? or of whose hand have I received any bribe to blind mine eyes therewith? and I will restore it you." Out of that whole assembled crowd there was not one who would have had the presumption to accuse the Saviour of having done him damage.

So far from this, they could but acknowledge that *He had even conferred great temporal blessings upon them.* O ravening multitude, has He not fed you when you were hungry? Did He not multiply the loaves and fishes for you? Did He not heal your lepers with His touch? cast out devils from your sons and daughters? raise up you paralytics? give sight to your blind, and open the ears of your deaf? For which of these good works do ye conspire to kill Him? Among that assembled multitude, there were doubtless some who owed to Him priceless boons, and yet, though all of them his debtors if they had known it, they clamour against Him as though He were the worst trouble of their lives, a pest and a pestilence to the place where He dwelt.

Was it His teaching that they complained of? Wherein did His teaching offend against morality? Wherein against the best interests of man? If you observe the teaching of Christ there was never any like it, even judge of by how far it would subserve human welfare. Here was the sum and substance of His doctrine, "Thou shalt love the Lord thy God with all thy heart, and thy neighbour as thyself." His precepts were of the mildest form. Did He bid them draw the sword and expel the Roman, or ride on in a ruthless career of carnage, and rapine? Did he stimulate them to let loose their unbridled passions? Did He tell them to seek first of all their own advantage and not to care for their neighbour's weal? Nay, every righteous state must own Him to be its best pillar, and the commonwealth of manhood must acknowledge Him to be its conservator; and yet, for all this, there they are, hounded on by their priests, seeking His blood, and crying, "Let him be crucified! let him be crucified!"

His whole intent evidently was their good. What did He preach for? No selfish motive could have been urged. Foxes had holes, and the birds of the air had nests, but He had not where to lay His head. The charity of a few of His disciples alone kept Him from absolute starvation. Cold mountains, and the midnight air, witnessed the fervour of His lonely prayers for the multitudes who are now hating Him. He lived for others: they could see this; they could not have observed Him during the three years of His ministry without saying, "Never lived there such an un-selfish soul as this"; they must have known, the most of them, and the rest might have known, had they enquired ever so little, that He had no object whatever in being here on earth, except that of seeking the good of men.

For which of these things do they clamour that He may be crucified? For which of His good works, for which of His generous words, for which of His holy deeds will they fasten His hands to the wood, and His feet to the tree? With unreasonable hatred, with senseless cruelty, they only answer to the question of Pilate, "Why, what evil hath he done?" "Let him be crucified! let him be crucified!" The true reason of their hate, no doubt, lay in the natural hatred of all men to perfect goodness. Man feels that the presence of goodness is a silent witness against his own sin, and therefore he longs to get rid of it. To be too holy in the judgment of men is a great crime, for it rebukes their sin. If the holy man has not the power of words, yet his life is one loud witness-bearing for God against the sins of his creatures. This inconvenient protesting led the wicked to desire the death of the holy and just One.

Besides, the priests were at their backs. It is a sad and lamentable thing, but it is often the case that the people are better than their religious teachers. No doubt bribery also was used in this case. Had not Rabbi Simon paid the multitude? Was there not a hope of some feast after the passover was over

to those who would use their throats against the Saviour?
Beside, there was the multitude going that way; and so if any
had compassion they held their tongue. Often they say that
"Discretion is the better part of valour;" and truly there must
be many valorous men, for they have much of valour's better
part, discretion. If they did not join in the shout, yet at least
they would not incommode the others, and so there was but one
cry, "Away with him! away with him! It is not fit that he
should live." What concentrated scorn there is in this fortieth
verse. It is not "this Jesus," they would not foul their mouths
with His name, but this *fellow*—"this devil," if you will. To
Barabbas they give the respect of mentioning his name; but
"this—" whom they hate so much, they will not even stoop
to mention. We have looked, then, at this great sin as it stands
in the history.

II. But now let us look, in the second place, AT THIS INCIDENT
AS SETTING FORTH THE SIN WHICH HAS BEEN THE GUILT OF THE
WORLD IN ALL AGES, AND WHICH IS THE WORLD'S GUILT NOW.

When the apostles went forth to preach the gospel, and the
truth had spread through many countries, there were severe
edicts passed by the Roman Emperors. Against whom were
these edicts framed? Against the foul offenders of that day?
It is well known that the whole Roman Empire was infested
with vices such as the cheek of modesty would blush to hear
named.

The first chapter of the Epistle to the Romans is a most
graphic picture of the state of society throughout the entire
Roman dominions. When severe laws were framed, why were
they not proclaimed against these atrocious vices? It is scarcely
fit that men should go unpunished who are guilty of crimes
such as the apostle Paul has mentioned, but I find no edicts
against these things—I find that they were borne with and
scarcely mentioned with censure; but burning, dragging at the
heels of wild horses, the sword, imprisonment, tortures of every
kind, were used against whom think you? Against the innocent,
humble followers of Christ, who, so far from defending themselves, were willing to suffer all these things, and presented
themselves like sheep at the shambles, willing to endure the
butcher's knife.

The cry of the world, under the persecutions of Imperial
Rome, was "Not Christ, but Sodomites, and murderers, and
thieves—we will bear with any of these, but not with Christ;
away with his followers from the earth." Then the world
changed its tactics; it became nominally Christian, and Anti-
christ came forth in all its blasphemous glory. The Pope of
Rome put on the triple crown, and called himself the Vicar

of Christ; then came in the abomination of the worship of saints, angels, images, and pictures; then came the mass, and I know not what, of detestable error; and what did the world say? "Popery for ever!" Down went every knee, and every head bowed before the sovereign representative of Peter at Rome. The world chose the harlot of Rome, and she who was drunk with the wine of her abominations had every eye to gaze upon her with admiration, while Christ's gospel was forgotten, buried in a few old books, and almost extinguished in darkness.

Since that day the world has changed its tactics yet again; in many parts of the earth Protestantism is openly acknowledged, and the gospel is preached, but what then? Then comes in Satan, and another Barabbas, the Barabbas of mere ceremonialism, and mere attendance at a place of worship is set up. So long as we are as good as our neighbours, and keep the outward rite, the inward does not matter. An outward name to live is set up, and is received by those who are dead; and many of you now present are quite easy and content, though you have never felt the quickening Spirit of God: though you have never been washed in the atoning blood, yet you are satisfied because you take a seat in some place of worship; you give your guinea, your donation to an hospital, or your subscription to a good object, forgetting and not caring to remember that all the making clean of the outside of the cup and the platter will never avail, unless the inward nature be renewed by the Spirit of the living God. This is the great Barabbas of the present age, and men prefer it before the Saviour.

That this is true, that the world really loves sin better than Christ, I think I could prove clearly enough by one simple fact. You have observed sometimes Christian men inconsistent, have you not? The inconsistency was nothing very great, if you had judged them according to ordinary rules of conduct. But you are well aware that a worldly man might commit any sin he liked, without much censure; but if the Christian man commits ever so little, then hands are held up, and the whole world cries, "Shame!" I do not want to have that altered, but I do want just to say this: "There is Mr. So-and-So, who is known to live a fast, wicked, gay life; well, I do not see that he is universally avoided and reprobated, but on the contrary, he is tolerated by most, and admired by some." But suppose a Christian man, a well-known professor, to have committed some fault which, compared with this, were not worth mentioning, and what is done? "Oh! publish it! publish it! Have you heard what Mr. So-and-So did? Have you heard of this hypocrite's transgression?" "Well, what was it?" You look at it: "Well, it is wrong, it is very wrong, but compared with what you say about it it is nothing at all."

The world therefore shows by the difference between the way in which it judges the professedly religious man, and that with which it judges its own, that it really can tolerate the most abandoned, but cannot tolerate the Christian. Of course, the Christian never will be altogether free from imperfections; the world's enmity is not against the Christian's imperfections evidently, because they will tolerate greater imperfections in others; the objection must therefore be against the man, against the profession which he has taken up, and the course which he desires to follow. Watch carefully, beloved, that ye give them no opportunity; but when ye see that the slightest mistake is laid hold of and exaggerated, in this you see a clear evidence that the world prefers Barabbas to the followers of the Lord Jesus Christ.

III. I come in the third place, and O for some assistance from on high, to observe that THE SIN OF PREFERRING BARABBAS TO CHRIST WAS THE SIN OF EVERY ONE OF US BEFORE OUR CONVERSION.

Will you turn over the leaves of your diary, now, dear friends, or fly upon the wings of memory to the hole of the pit whence you were digged. Did you not, O you who live close to Christ, did you not once despise Him? What company did you like best? Was it not that of the frivolous, if not that of the profane? When you sat with God's people, their talk was very tedious; if they spoke of divine realities, and of experimental subjects, you did not understand them, you felt them to be troublesome. I can look back upon some whom I know now to be most venerable believers, whom I thought to be a gross nuisance when I heard them talk of the things of God. What were our thoughts about? When we had time for thinking, what were our favourite themes? Not much did we meditate upon eternity; not much upon Him who came to deliver us from the misery of hell's torments.

Brethren, His great love wherewith He loved us was never laid to heart by us as it should have been; nay, if we read the story of the crucifixion, it had no more effect upon our mind than a common tale. We knew not the beauties of Christ; we thought of any trifle sooner than of Him. And what were our pleasures? When we had what we called a day's enjoyment, where did we seek it? At the foot of the cross? In the service of the Saviour? In communion with Him? Far from it; the further we could remove from godly associations the better pleased we were. Some of us have to confess with shame that we were never more in our element than when we were without a conscience, when conscience ceased to accuse us and we could plunge into sin with riot.

What was our reading then? any book sooner than the Bible: and if there had lain in our way anything that would have exalted Christ and extolled Him in our understandings, we should have put by the book as much too dry to please us. Any three-volume heap of nonsense, any light literature; nay, perhaps, even worse would have delighted our eye and our heart; but thoughts of *His* eternal delight towards us—thoughts of His matchless passion and His glory now in heaven, never came across our minds, nor would we endure those who would have led us to such meditations.

What were our aspirations then? We were looking after business, aiming at growing rich, famous for learning or admired for ability. Self was what we lived for. If we had some regard for others, and some desire to benefit our race, yet self was at the bottom of it all. We did not live for God—we could not honestly say, as we woke in the morning, "I hope to live for God to-day"; at night, we could not look back upon the day, and say, "We have this day served God." He was not in all our thoughts. Where did we spend our best praise? Did we praise Christ? No; we praised cleverness, and when it was in association with sin, we praised it none the less. We admired those who could most fully minister to our own fleshly delights, and felt the greatest love to those who did us the worst injury. Is not this our confession as we review the past? Have I not read the very history of your life? I know I have of my own. Alas! for those dark days, in which our besotted soul went after any evil, but would not follow after Christ.

It would have been the same to-day with us, if almighty grace had not made the difference. We may as well expect the river to cease to run to the sea, as expect the natural man to turn from the current of his sins. As well might we expect fire to become water, or water to become fire, as for the unrenewed heart ever to love Christ. It was mighty grace which made us to seek the Saviour. And as we look back upon our past lives, it must be with mingled feelings of gratitude for the change, and of sorrow that we should have been so grossly foolish as to have chosen Barabbas, and have said of the Saviour, "Let him be crucified!"

IV. And now I shall come to the closing part of the sermon, which is, THAT THERE ARE DOUBTLESS MANY HERE WHO THIS DAY PREFER BARABBAS TO OUR LORD JESUS CHRIST.

Let me first state your case, dear friends. I would describe it honestly, but at the same time so describe it that you will see your sin in it; and while I am doing so, my object will be to expostulate with you, if haply the Lord may change your will. There are many here, I fear, who prefer sin to Christ. There stands drunkenness, I see it mirrored before me with all its folly, its witlessness, its greed and filth; but the man chooses all that, and though he has known by head knowledge something concerning the beauty and excellency of Christ, he virtually says of Jesus, "Not this man, but drunkenness."

Then there are other cases, where a favourite lust reigns supreme in their hearts. The men know the evil of the sin, and they have good cause to know it; they know also something of the sweetness of religion, for they are never happier than when they come up with God's people; and they go home sometimes from a solemn sermon, especially if it touches their vice, and they feel, "God has spoken to my soul to-day, and I am brought to a standstill." But for all that, the temptation comes again, and they fall as they have fallen before. I am afraid there are some of you whom no arguments will ever move; you have become so set on this mischief, that it will be your eternal ruin. But oh! think you, how will this look when you are in hell—"I preferred that foul Barabbas of lust to the beauties and perfections of the Saviour, who came into the world to seek and to save that which was lost!" and yet this is the case, not of some, but of a great multitude who listen to the gospel, and yet prefer sin to its saving power.

There may be some here, too, of another class, who prefer *gain*. It has come to this: if they become truly the Lord's people, they cannot do in trade what they now think their trade requires them to do; if they become really and genuinely believers, they must of course become honest, but their trade would not pay, they say, if it were conducted upon honest principles; or it is such a trade, and there are some few such, as ought not to be conducted at all, much less by Christians. Here comes the turning-point. Shall I take the gold, or shall I take Christ? True, it is cankered gold, and gold on which a curse must come. It is the fool's pence, may be it is gain that is extorted from the miseries of the poor; is money that would not ever stand the light because it is not fairly come by; money that will burn its way right through your souls when you get upon your death-beds; but yet men who love the world, say, "No, not Christ, give me a full purse, and away with Christ." Others, less base or less honest, cry, "We know His excellence, we wish we could have Him, but we cannot have Him on terms which involve the renunciation of our dearly-beloved gain." "Not this man, but Barabbas."

I might thus multiply instances, but the same principle runs through them all. If anything whatever keeps you back from giving your heart to the Lord Jesus Christ, you are guilty of setting up an opposition candidate to Christ in your soul, and you are choosing "not this man, but Barabbas."

Let me occupy a few minutes with pleading Christ's cause with you. Why is it that you reject Christ? Are you not conscious of the many good things which you receive from Him? You would have been dead if it had not been for Him; nay, worse than that, you would have been in hell. God has sharpened the great axe; justice, like a stern woodman, stood with the axe uplifted, ready to cut you down as a cumberer of the ground. A hand was seen stopping the arm of the avenger, and a voice was heard saying, "Let it alone, till I dig about it and dung it." Who was it that appeared just then in your moment of extremity? It was no other than that Christ, of whom you think so little that you prefer drunkenness or vice to Him! You are this day in the house of God, listening to a discourse which I hope is sent from Him. You might have been in hell— think one moment of that—shut out from hope, enduring in body and soul unutterable pangs. That you are not there, should make you love and bless Him, who has said, "Deliver him from going down into the pit." Why will you prefer your own gain and self-indulgence to that blessed One to whom you owe so much. Common gratitude should make you deny yourself something for Him who denied Himself so much that He might bless you.

Do I hear you say that you cannot follow Christ, because His precepts are too severe? In what respect are they too severe? If you yourself were set to judge them, what is the point with which you would find fault? They deny you your sins—say, they deny you your miseries. They do not permit you, in fact, to ruin yourself. There is no precept of Christ which is not for your good, and there is nothing which He forbids you which He does not forbid on the principle that it would harm you to indulge in it. But suppose Christ's precepts to be ever so stern, is it not better that you should put up with them than be ruined?

The soldier submits implicitly to the captain's command, because he knows that without discipline there can be no victory, and the whole army may be cut in pieces if there be a want of order. When the sailor has risked his life to penetrate through the thick ice of the north, we find him consenting to all the orders and regulations of authority, and bearing all the hardships of the adventure, because he is prompted by the desire of assisting in a great discovery, or stimulated by a large reward. And surely the little self-denials which Christ calls us to will be abundantly recompensed by the reward He offers; and when the soul and its eternal interests are at stake, we may well put up

c

with these temporary inconveniences if we may inherit eternal life.

I think I hear you say that you would be a Christian, but there is no happiness in it. I would not tell you a falsehood on this point, I would speak the truth if it were so, but I do solemnly declare that there is more joy in the Christian life than there is in any other form of life; that if I had to die like a dog, and there were no hereafter, I would prefer to be a Christian. You shall appeal to the very poorest among us, to those who are most sick and most despised, and they will tell you the same. There is not an old country woman shivering in her old ragged red cloak over a handful of fire, full of rheumatism, with an empty cupboard and an aged body, who would change with the very highest and greatest of you if she had to give up her religion; no, she would tell you that her Redeemer was a greater comfort to her than all the luxuries which could be heaped upon the tables of Dives.

You make a mistake when you dream that my Master does not make His disciples blessed; they are a blessed people who put their trust in Christ. Still I think I hear you say, "Yes, this is all very well, but still I prefer *present* pleasure." Dost thou not in this talk like a child; nay, like a fool, for what is present pleasure? How long does that word "present" last? If thou couldst have ten thousand years of merriment I might agree with thee in a measure, but even there I should have but short patience with thee, for what would be ten thousand years of sin's merriment compared with millions upon millions of years of sin's penalty.

Why, at the longest, your life will be but very short. Are you not conscious that time flies more hurriedly every day? As you grow older, do you not seem as if you had lived a shorter time instead of longer? till, perhaps, if you could live to be as old as Jacob, you would say, "Few and evil have my days been, for they appear fewer as they grow more numerous." You know that this life is but a span, and is soon over. Look to the graveyards, see how they are crowded with green mounds. Remember your own companions, how one by one they have passed away. They were as firm and strong as you, but they have gone like a shadow that declineth. Is it worth while to have this snatch space of pleasure, and then to lie down in eternal pain? I pray you to answer this question. Is it worth while to choose Barabbas for the sake of the temporary gain he may give you, and give up Christ, and so renounce the eternal treasures of joy and happiness which are at His right hand for evermore?

Many men profess to be believers in Scripture, and yet, when you come to the point as to whether they do believe in eternal woe and eternal joy, there is a kind of something inside which whispers, "That is in the Book—but still it is not real, it is not true to us." Make it true to yourselves, and when you have so done it, and have clearly proved that you must be in happiness or woe, and that you must here either have Barabbas for your master, or have Christ for your Lord, then, I say, like sane men, judge which is the better choice, and may God's mighty grace give you spiritual sanity to make the right choice; but this I know, you never will unless that mighty Spirit who alone leads us to choose the right, and reject the wrong, shall come upon you and lead you to fly to a Saviour's wounds.

I need not, I think, prolong the service now, but I hope you will prolong it at your own houses by thinking of the matter. And may I put the question personally to all as you separate, whose are you? On whose side are you? There are no neuters; there are no betweenites: you either serve Christ or Belial; you are either with the Lord or with His enemies. Who is on the Lord's side this day? Who? Who is for Christ and for His cross; for His blood, and for His throne? Who, on the other hand, are His foes? As many as are not for Christ, are numbered with His enemies. Be not so numbered any longer, for the gospel comes to you with an inviting voice—"Believe in the Lord Jesus Christ, and thou shalt be saved." God help thee to believe and cast thyself upon Him now; if and thou trustest Him, thou art saved now, and thou shalt be saved for ever. Amen.

"THE PRECIOUS BLOOD OF CHRIST"

A Sermon

Text.—"The precious blood of Christ."—1 Peter i. 19.

BLOOD has from the beginning been regarded by God as a most precious thing. He has hedged about this fountain of vitality with the most solemn sanctions. The Lord thus commanded Noah and his descendants, "Flesh with the life thereof, which is the blood thereof, shall ye not eat." Man had every moving thing that liveth given him for meat, but they were by no means to eat the blood with the flesh. Things strangled were to be considered unfit for food, since God would not have man become too familiar with blood by eating or drinking it in any shape or form. Even the blood of bulls and goats thus had a sacredness put upon it by God's decrees.

As for the blood of man, you remember how God's threatening ran, "And surely your blood of your lives will I require; at the hand of every beast will I require it, and at the hand of man; at the hand of every man's brother will I require the life of man. Whoso sheddeth man's blood, by man shall his blood be shed: for in the image of God made he man."

It is true that the first murderer had not his blood shed by man, but then the crime was new and the penalty had not then been settled and proclaimed, and therefore the case was clearly exceptional, and one by itself; and, moreover, Cain's doom was probably far more terrible than if he had been slain upon the spot: he was permitted to fill up his measure of wickedness, to be a wanderer and a vagabond upon the face of the earth, and then to enter into the dreadful heritage of wrath, which his life of sin had doubtless greatly increased. Under the theocratic dispensation, in which God was the King and governed Israel, murder was always punished in the most exemplary manner, and there was never any toleration or excuse for it. Eye for eye, tooth for tooth, life for life, was the stern inexorable law. It is expressly written, "Ye shall take no satisfaction for the life of a murderer which is guilty of death: but he shall surely be put to death."

Even in cases where life was taken in chance-medley or misadventure, the matter was not overlooked. The slayer fled at once to the city of refuge, where, after having his case properly

32

tried, he was allowed to reside; but there was no safety for him elsewhere until the death of the high priest. The general law in all cases was, "So ye shall not pollute the land wherein ye are: for blood it defileth the land: and the land cannot be cleansed of the blood that is shed therein, but by the blood of him that shed it. Defile not therefore the land which ye shall inhabit, wherein I dwell: for I the Lord dwell among the children of Israel."

It is clear, then, that blood was ever precious in God's sight, and He would have it so in ours.

Now, if in ordinary cases the shedding of life be thus precious, can you guess how fully God utters His heart's meaning when He says, "Precious in the sight of the Lord is the death *of his saints?*" If the death of a rebel be precious, what must be the death of a child? If He will not contemplate the shedding of the blood of His own enemies and of them that curse Him without proclaiming vengeance, what think you concerning His own elect, of whom He says, "Precious shall their blood be in his sight?" Will He not avenge them, though He bear long with them? Shall the cup which the harlot of Rome filled with the blood of the saints, long remain unavenged? Shall not the martyrs from Piedmont and the Alps, and from our Smithfield, and from the hills of covenanting Scotland, yet obtain from God the vengeance due for all that they suffered, and all the blood which they poured forth in the defence of His cause?

I have taken you up, you see, from the *beast* to *man*, from man to *God's chosen* men, the martyrs. I have another step to indicate to you: it is a far longer one—it is to the blood of JESUS CHRIST. Here, powers of speech would fail to convey to you an idea of the preciousness! Behold here, a person innocent, without taint within, or flaw without; a Person meritorious, who magnified the law and made it honourable—a Person who served both God and man even unto death. Nay, here you have a divine Person—so divine, that in the Acts of the Apostles Paul calls His blood the "blood of God." Place innocence, and merit, and dignity, and position, and Godhead itself, in the scale, and then conceive what must be the inestimable value of the blood which Jesus Christ poured forth. Angels must have seen that matchless bloodshedding with wonder and amazement, and even God Himself saw what never before was seen in creation or in providence; He saw Himself more gloriously displayed than in the whole universe beside.

Let us come nearer to the text and try to shew forth the preciousness of the blood of Christ. We shall confine ourselves to an enumeration of some of the many properties possessed by this precious blood. I felt as I was studying, that I should have so many divisions this morning, that some of you would compare my sermon to the bones in Ezekiel's vision,—they were very many and they were very dry; but I am in hopes that God's Holy Spirit may so descend upon the bones in my sermon, which would be but dry of themselves, that they being quickened and full of life, you may admire the exceeding great army of God's thoughts of loving-kindness towards His people, in the sacrifice of His own dear Son.

The precious blood of Christ is useful to God's people in a thousand ways: we intend to speak of twelve of them. After all, the real preciousness of a thing in the time of pinch and trial, must depend upon its usefulness. A bag of pearls would be to us, this morning, far more precious than a bag of bread; but you have all heard the story of the man in the desert, who stumbled, when near to die, upon a bag, and opened it, hoping that it might be the wallet of some passer-by, and he found in it *nothing but pearls!* If they had been crusts of bread, how much more precious would they have been! I say, in the hour of necessity and peril, the use of a thing really constitutes the preciousness of it. This may not be according to political economy, but it is according to common sense.

1. The precious blood of Christ has a REDEEMING POWER. It redeems from the law. We were all under the law which says, "This do, and live." We were slaves to it: Christ has paid the ransom price, and the law is no longer our tyrant master. We are entirely free from it. The law had a dreadful curse; it threatened that whosoever should violate one of its precepts, should die: "Christ hath redeemed us from the curse of the law, being made a curse for us." By the fear of this curse, the law inflicted a continual dread on those who were under it; they knew they had disobeyed it, and they were all their lifetime subject to bondage, fearful lest death and destruction should come upon them at any moment: but we are not under the law, but under grace, and consequently "We have not received the spirit of bondage again to fear, but we have received the spirit of adoption, whereby we cry, Abba, Father."

We are not afraid of the law now; its worst thunders cannot affect us, for they are not hurled at us! Its most tremendous lightnings cannot touch us, for we are sheltered beneath the cross of Christ, where the thunder loses its terror and the lightning its fury. We read the law of God with pleasure now; we look upon it as in the ark covered with the mercy seat, and not thundering in tempests from Sinai's fiery brow.

Happy is that man who knows his full redemption from the law, its curse, its penalty, its present dread. My brethren, the life of a Jew, happy as it was compared with that of a heathen, was perfect drudgery compared to yours and mine. He was hedged in with a thousand commands and prohibitions, his forms and ceremonies were abundant, and their details minutely arranged. He was always in danger of making himself unclean. If he sat upon a bed or upon a stool, he might be defiled; if he drank out of an earthen pitcher, or even touched the wall of a house, a leprous man might have put his hand there before him, and he would thus become defiled.

A thousand sins of ignorance were like so many hidden pits in his way; he must be perpetually in fear lest he should be cut off from the people of God. When he had done his best any one day, he knew he had not finished; no Jew could ever talk of a finished work. The bullock was offered, but he must bring another; the lamb was offered this morning, but another must be offered this evening, another to-morrow, and another the next day. The Passover is celebrated with holy rites; it must be kept in the same manner next year. The high priest has gone within the veil once, but he must go there again; the thing is never finished, it is always beginning. He never comes any nearer to the end. "The law could not make the comer thereunto perfect."

But see *our* position: we are redeemed from this. Our law is fulfilled, for Christ is the end of the law for righteousness; our passover is slain, for Jesus died; our righteousness is finished, for we are complete in Him; our victim is slain, our priest has gone within the veil, the blood is sprinkled; we are clean, and clean beyond any fear of defilement, "For he hath perfected for ever those that were set apart." Value this precious blood, my beloved, because thus it has redeemed you from the thraldom and bondage which the law imposed upon its votaries.

2. The value of the blood lies much in its ATONING EFFICACY. We are told in Leviticus, that "it is the blood which maketh an atonement for the soul." God never forgave sin apart from blood under the law. This stood as a constant text—"Without shedding of blood there is no remission." Meal and honey, sweet spices and incense, would not avail without shedding of blood. There was no remission promised to future diligence or deep repentance; without shedding of blood pardon never came. The blood, and the blood alone put away sin, and permitted that man to come to God's courts to worship, because it made him one with God. The blood is the great at-one-ment. There is no hope of pardon for the sin of any man, except through its punishment being fully endured. God must punish sin. It is not an arbitrary arrangement that sin shall be punished, but it is a part of the very constitution of moral government that sin

must be punished. Never did God swerve from that, and never will He. "He will by no means clear the guilty."

Christ, therefore, came and was punished in the place and stead of all His people. Ten thousand times ten thousand are the souls for whom Jesus shed His blood. He, for the sins of all the elect, hath a complete atonement made. For every man of Adam born, who has believed or shall believe on that, or who is taken to glory before being capable of believing, Christ has made a complete atonement; and there is none other plan by which sinners can be made at one with God, except by Jesus' precious blood. I may make sacrifices; I may mortify my body; I may be baptized; I may receive sacraments; I may pray until my knees grow hard with kneeling; I may read devout words until I know them by heart; I may celebrate masses; I may worship in one language or in fifty languages; but I can never be at one with God, except by blood; and that blood, "the precious blood of Christ."

My dear friends, many of you have felt the power of Christ's redeeming blood; you are not under the law now, but under grace: you have also felt the power of the atoning blood; you know that you are reconciled unto God by the death of His Son; you feel that He is no angry God to you, that He loves you with a love unchangeable; but this is not the case with you all. O that it were! I do pray that you may know this very day the atoning power of the blood of Jesus. Creature, wouldst thou not be at one with thy Creator? Puny man, wouldst thou not have Almighty God to be thy friend? Thou canst not be at one with God except through the at-one-ment. God hath set forth Christ to be a propitiation for our sins. Oh, take the propitiation through faith in His blood, and be thou at one with God.

3. Thirdly, the precious blood of Jesus Christ has A CLEANSING POWER. John tells us in his first Epistle, first chapter, seventh verse, "The blood of Jesus Christ his Son, cleanseth us from all sin." Sin has a directly defiling effect upon the sinner, hence the need of cleansing. Suppose that God the Holy One were perfectly willing to be at one with an unholy sinner, which is supposing a case that cannot be, yet even should the pure eyes of the Most High wink at sin, still as long as we are unclean we never could feel in our own hearts anything like joy, and rest, and peace. Sin is a plague to the man who has it, as well as a hateful thing to the God who abhors it. I must be made clean, I must have mine iniquities washed away, or I never can be happy. The first mercy that is sung of in the one hundred and third Psalm is, "Who forgiveth all thine iniquities."

Now we know it is by the precious blood that sin is cleansed. Murder, adultery, theft, whatever the sin may be, there is power in the veins of Christ to take it away at once and for ever. No matter how many, nor how deeply-seated our offences may be, the blood cries, "Though your sins be as scarlet, they shall be as white as snow; though they be red like crimson, they shall be as wool." It is the song of heaven,—"We have washed our robes and made them white in the blood of the Lamb." This is the experience of earth, for none was ever cleansed except in this fountain, opened for the house of David for sin and for uncleanness.

You have heard this so often that perhaps if an angel told it to you, you would not take much interest in it, except you have known experimentally the horror of uncleanness and the blessedness of being made clean. Beloved, it is a thought which ought to make our hearts leap within us, that through Jesus' blood there is not a spot left upon any believer, not a wrinkle nor any such thing. Oh precious blood, removing the hell-stains of abundant iniquity, and permitting me to stand accepted in the beloved, notwithstanding all the many ways in which I have rebelled against my God!

4. A fourth property of the blood of Christ is ITS PRESERVING POWER. You will rightly comprehend this when you remember the dreadful night of Egypt, when the destroying angel was abroad to slay God's enemies. A bitter cry went up from house to house as the firstborn of all Egypt, from Pharaoh on the throne to the firstborn of the woman behind the mill and the slave in the dungeon, fell dead in a moment. The angel sped with noiseless wing through every street of Egypt's many cities; but there were some houses which he could not enter: he sheathed his sword and breathed no malediction there. What was it which preserved the houses? The inhabitants were not better than others, their habitations were not more elegantly built, there was nothing except the bloodstain on the lintel and on the two side posts, and it is written, "When I see the blood I will pass over you."

There was nothing whatever which gained the passover for Israel but just the sprinkling of blood. The father of the house had taken a lamb and killed it, had caught the blood in a bason, and while the lamb was roasted that it might be eaten by every inhabitant of the house, he took a bunch of hyssop, stirred the bason of blood and went outside with his children and began to strike the posts, and to strike the door, and as soon as this was done, they were all safe, all safe: no angel could touch them, the fiends of hell themselves could not venture there.

Beloved, see, we are preserved in Christ Jesus. Did not God see the blood before you and I saw it, and was not that the reason why He spared our forfeited lives when like barren fig trees, we brought forth no fruit for Him? When we saw the blood, let us remember it was not our seeing it, which really saved it; one sight of it gave us peace, but it was God's seeing it that saved us. "When *I* see the blood I will pass over you." And to-day, if my eye of faith be dim, and I can scarce see the precious blood, so as to rejoice that I am washed in it, yet God can see the blood, and as long as the undimmed eye of Jehovah looks upon the atoning sacrifice of the Lord Jesus, He cannot smite one soul that is covered with its scarlet mantle.

Oh, how precious is this blood-red shield! My soul, cower thou down under it when the darts of hell are flying: this is the chariot, the covering whereof is of purple; let the storm come, and the deluge rise, let even the fiery hail descend, beneath that crimson pavilion my soul must rest secure, for what can touch me, when I am covered with *His* precious blood?

Let me ask you to get here, right under the shelter of the cross. Sit down now beneath the shadow of the cross and feel, "I am safe, I am safe, O ye devils of hell; or ye angels of God—I could challenge you all, and say, 'Who shall separate me from the love of God in Christ Jesus, or who shall lay anything to my charge, seeing that Christ hath died for me.'" When heaven is on a blaze, when earth begins to shake, when the mountains rock, when God divides the righteous from the wicked, happy will they be who can find a shelter beneath the blood. But where will you be who have never trusted in its cleansing power? You will call to the rocks to hide you, and to the mountains to cover you, but all in vain. God help you now, or even the blood will not help you then.

5. Fifthly, the blood of Christ is precious because of its PLEAD-ING PREVALENCE. Paul says in the twelfth chapter of his Epistle to the Hebrews, at the twenty-fourth verse, "It speaketh better things than that of Abel." Abel's blood pleaded and prevailed; its cry was "Vengeance" and Cain was punished. Jesus' blood pleads and prevails; its cry is "Father, forgive them!" and sinners are forgiven through it. When I cannot pray as I would, how sweet to remember that the blood prays! There is no voice in my tongue, but there is always a voice in the blood. If I cannot, when I bow before my God, get farther than to say "God be merciful to me, a sinner," yet my advocate before the throne is not dumb because *I* am, and his plea has not lost its power because my faith in it may happen to be diminished.

The blood is always alike prevalent with God. The wounds of Jesus are so many mouths to plead with God for sinners—what if I say they are so many chains with which love is led captive, and sovereign mercy bound to bless every favoured child? What if I say that the wounds of Jesus have become donors of grace through which divine love comes forth to the vilest of the vile, and doors through which our wants go up to God and plead with Him that He would be pleased to supply them? Next time you cannot pray, next time you are crying and striving and groaning up in that upper room, praise the value of the precious blood which maketh intercession before the eternal throne.

6. Sixthly, the blood is precious where perhaps we little expect it to operate. It is precious, because of its MELTING INFLUENCE on the human heart. "They shall look upon me whom they have pierced, and they shall mourn for him, as one that mourneth for his only son, and shall be in bitterness for him, as one that is in bitterness for his firstborn." There is a great complaint among sinners, when they are a little awakened, that they feel their hearts so hard. The blood is a mighty melter. Alchemists of old sought after a universal solvent: the blood of Jesus is that. There is no nature so stubborn that a sight of the love of God in Christ Jesus cannot melt it, if grace shall open the blind eye to see Christ. The stone in the human heart shall melt away, when it is plunged into a bath of blood divine. Cannot you say, dear friends, that Toplady was right in his hymn—

> "Law and terrors do but harden
> All the while they work alone,
> But a sense of blood-bought pardon,
>   Soon dissolves a heart of stone."

Sinner, if God shall lead thee to believe this morning in Christ to save thee; if thou wilt trust thy soul in His hands to have it saved, that hard heart of thine will melt at once. You would think differently of sin, my friends, if you knew that Christ smarted for it. Oh! if you knew that out of those dear languid eyes, there looked the loving heart of Jesus upon you, I know you would say, "I hate the sin that made him mourn, and fastened him to the accursed tree." I do not think that preaching the law generally softens men's hearts. Hitting men with a hard hammer may often drive the particles of a hard heart more closely together, and make the iron yet more hard; but oh, to preach Christ's love—His great love wherewith He loved us even when we were dead in sins, and to tell to sinners that there is life in a look at the crucified One—surely this will prove that Christ was exalted on high to give repentance and remission of sins. Come for repentance, if you cannot come repenting. Come *for* a broken heart, if you cannot come *with* a broken heart. Come to be melted, if you are not melted. Come to be wounded, if you are not wounded.

7. But then comes in a seventh property of the precious blood. The same blood that melts has A GRACIOUS POWER TO PACIFY.

John Bunyan speaks of the law as coming to sweep a chamber like a maid with a broom; and when she began to sweep there was a great dust which almost choked people, and got into their eyes; but then came the gospel with its drops of water, and laid the dust, and then the broom might be used far better. Now it sometimes happens that the law of God makes such a dust in the sinner's soul, that nothing but the precious blood of Jesus Christ can make that dust lie still. The sinner is so disquieted that nothing can ever give him any relief except to know that Jesus died for him.

When I felt the burden of my sin, I do confess all the preaching I ever heard never gave me one single atom of comfort. I was told to do this and to do that, and when I had done it all, I had not advanced one inch the farther. I thought I must feel something, or pray a certain quantity; and when I had done that, the burden was quite as heavy. But the moment I saw that there was nothing whatever for me to do, that Jesus did it long, long ago, that all my sins were put on His back and that He suffered all I ought to have suffered, why then my heart had peace with God, peace by believing, peace through the precious blood.

Two soldiers were on duty in the citadel of Gibraltar, one of them had obtained peace through the precious blood of Christ, the other was in very great distress of mind. It happened to be their turn to stand, both of them, sentinel the same night; and there are many long passages in the rock, which passages are adapted to convey sounds a very great distance. The soldier in distress of mind was ready to beat his breast for grief: he felt he had rebelled against God, and could not find how he could be reconciled; when, suddenly, there came through the air what seemed to him to be a mysterious voice from heaven saying these words, "The precious blood of Christ." In a moment he saw it all: it was that which reconciled us to God; and he rejoiced with joy unspeakable and full of glory.

Now did those words come directly from God? No. They did as far as the effect was concerned—they did come from the Holy Spirit. Who was it that had spoken those words? Curiously enough, the other sentinel at the far end of the passage was standing still and meditating, when an officer came by and it was his duty of course to give the word for the night, and with soldier-like promptitude he did give it, but not accurately, for instead of giving the proper word, he was so taken up by his meditations that he said to the officer, "The precious blood of Christ." He corrected himself in a moment, but however, he had said it, and it had passed along the passage and reached the ear for which God meant it, and the man found peace and spent his life in the fear of God, being in after years the means of completing one of our excellent translations of the Word of God into the Hindoo language.

Who can tell, dear friends, how much peace you may give by only telling the story of our Saviour. If I only had about a dozen words to speak and knew I must die, I would say, "This is a faithful saying and worthy of all acceptation, that Christ Jesus came into the world to save sinners." The doctrine of substitution is the pith and marrow of the gospel, and if you can hold that forth, you will prove the value of the precious blood by its peace-giving power.

8. We can only spare a minute now upon ITS SANCTIFYING INFLUENCE. The apostle tells us in the ninth chapter and the fourteenth verse that Christ sanctified the people by His own blood. Certain it is, that the same blood which justifies by taking away sin, does in its after-action act upon the new nature and lead it onward to subdue sin and to follow out the command of God. There is no motive for holiness so great as that which streams from the veins of Jesus. If you want to know why you should be obedient to God's will, my brethren, go and look upon Him who sweat, as it were, great drops of blood, and the love of Christ will constrain you, because you will thus judge, "That if one died for all, then were all dead: and that he died for all, that we which live might not henceforth live unto ourselves, but unto him that died for us and rose again."

9. In the ninth place, another blessed property of the blood of Jesus, is ITS POWER TO GIVE ENTRANCE. We are told that the high priest never went within the veil without blood; and surely we can never get into God's heart, nor into the secret of the Lord, which is with them that fear Him, nor into any familiar intercourse with our great Father and Friend, except by the sprinkling of the precious blood of Jesus. "We have access with boldness into this grace wherein we stand," but we never dare go a step towards God, except as we are sprinkled with this precious blood. I am persuaded some of us do not come near to God, because we forget the blood. If you try to have fellowship with God in your graces, your experiences, your believings, you will fail; but if you try to come near to God as you stand in Christ Jesus, you will have courage to come; and on the other hand, God will run to meet you when He sees you in the face of His anointed. Oh, for power to get near to God! But there is no getting near to God, except as we get near to the cross. Praise the blood, then, for its power of giving you nearness to God.

10. Tenthly—a hint only. The blood is very precious, in the tenth place, for ITS CONFIRMING POWER. No covenant, we are told, was ever valid, unless victims were slain and blood sprinkled;

and it is the blood of Jesus which has ratified the new covenant, and made its promises sure to all the seed. Hence it is called "the blood of the everlasting covenant." The apostle changes the figure, and he says that a testament is not of force, except the testator be dead. The blood is a proof that the testator died, and now the law holds good to every legatee, because Jesus Christ has signed it with His own gore. Beloved, let us rejoice that the promises are yea and amen, for no other reason than this, because Christ Jesus died and rose again. Had there been no bowing of the head upon the tree, no slumbering in the sepulchre, no rising from the tomb, then the promises had been uncertain fickle things, not "immutable things wherein it is impossible for God to lie," and consequently they could never have afforded strong consolation to those who have fled for refuge to Christ Jesus. See then the confirming nature of the blood of Jesus and count it very precious.

11. I have almost done; but there remains another, it is the eleventh one, and that is THE INVIGORATING POWER of the precious blood. If you want to know that, you must see it set forth as we often do when we cover the table with the white cloth and put thereon the bread and wine. What mean we by this ordinance? We mean by it, that Christ suffered for us, and that we being already washed in His precious blood and so made clean, do come to the table to drink wine as an emblem of the way in which we live and feed upon His body and upon His blood. He tells us "Except a man shall eat my flesh and drink my blood, there is no life in him." We do therefore, after a spiritual sort, drink His blood, and He says "My blood is drink indeed." Superior drink! Transcendent drink! Strengthening drink— such drink as angels never taste though they drink before the eternal throne.

Oh beloved, whenever your spirit faints, this wine shall comfort you; when your griefs are many, drink and forget your misery, and remember your sufferings no more. When you are very weak and faint, take not *a little* of this for your soul's sake, but drink *a full draught* of the wine on the lees, well refined, which was set abroach by the soldier's spike, and flowed from Christ's own heart. "Drink to the full; yea, drink abundantly O beloved," saith Christ to the spouse; and do not thou linger when He invites. You see the blood has power without to cleanse, and then it has power within to strengthen. O precious blood, how many are thy uses! May I prove them all!

12. Lastly, and twelfthly—twelve is the number of perfection. We have brought out a perfect number of its uses—the blood has AN OVERCOMING POWER. It is written in the Revelation, "They overcame through the blood of the Lamb." How could

they do otherwise? He that fights with the precious blood of Jesus fights with a weapon that will cut through soul and spirit, joints and marrow, a weapon that makes hell tremble, and makes heaven subservient, and earth obedient to the will of the men who can wield it. The blood of Jesus! sin dies at its presence, death ceases to be death: hell itself would be dried up if that blood could operate there. The blood of Jesus! heaven's gates are opened; bars of iron are pushed back. The blood of Jesus! my doubts and fears flee, my troubles and disasters disappear. The blood of Jesus! shall I not go on conquering and to conquer so long as I can plead that! In heaven this shall be the choice jewel which shall glitter upon the head of Jesus—that He gives to His people "Victory, victory, through the blood of the Lamb."

And now, is this blood to be had? Can it be got at? Yes, it is free, as well as full of virtue,—free to every soul that believeth. Whosoever careth to come and trust in Jesus shall find the virtue of this blood in his case this very morning. Away from your own works and doings. Turn those eyes of yours to the full atonement made, to the utmost ransom paid; and if God enables thee, poor soul, this morning to say, "I take that precious blood to be my only hope," you are saved, and you may sing with the rest of us

"Now freed from sin, I walk at large;
The Saviour's blood's my full discharge,
At His dear feet my soul I'll lay,
A sinner saved, and homage pay."

God grant it may be so, for His name's sake. Amen.

MOURNING AT THE SIGHT OF THE CRUCIFIED

A Sermon

Text.—"And all the people that came together to that sight, beholding the things which were done, smote their breasts, and returned."—
Luke xxiii. 48.

MANY in that crowd came together to behold the crucifixion of
Jesus, in a condition of the most furious malice. They had
hounded the Saviour as dogs pursue a stag, and at last, all mad
with rage, they hemmed Him in for death. Others, willing
enough to spend an idle hour, and to gaze upon a sensational
spectacle, swelled the mob until a vast assembly congregated
around the little hill upon which the three crosses were raised.
There unanimously, whether of malice or of wantonness, they
all joined in mockery of the Victim who hung upon the centre
cross. Some thrust out the tongue, some wagged their heads,
others scoffed and jeered, some taunted Him in words, and
others in signs, but all alike exulted over the defenceless Man
who was given as a prey to their teeth.

Earth never beheld a scene in which so much unrestrained
derision and expressive contempt were poured upon one man so
unanimously and for so long a time. It must have been hideous
to the last degree to have seen so many grinning faces and mocking eyes, and to have heard so many cruel words and scornful
shouts. The spectacle was too detestable to be long endured
of heaven. Suddenly the sun, shocked at the scene, veiled his
face, and for three long hours the ribald crew sat shivering in
midday midnight. Meanwhile the earth trembled beneath their
feet, the rocks were rent, and the temple, in superstitious defence
of whose perpetuity they had committed the murder of the just,
had its holy veil rent as though by strong invisible hands.

The news of this, and the feeling of horror produced by the
darkness, and the earth-tremor, caused a revulsion of feelings;
there were no more gibes and jests, no more thrustings out of
the tongue and cruel mockeries, but they went their way solitary
and alone to their homes, or in little silent groups, while each
man after the manner of Orientals when struck with sudden awe,
smote upon his breast. Far different was the procession to the
gates of Jerusalem from that march of madness which had come

44

out therefrom. Observe the power which God hath over human minds! See how He can tame the wildest, and make the most malicious and proud to cower down at His feet when He doth but manifest Himself in the wonders of nature! How much more cowed and terrified will they be when He makes bare His arm and comes forth in the judgments of His wrath to deal with them according to their deserts!

This sudden and memorable change in so vast a multitude is the apt representative of two other remarkable mental changes. How like it is to the gracious transformation which a sight of the cross has often worked most blessedly in the hearts of men! Many have come under the sound of the gospel resolved to scoff, but they have returned to pray. The idlest and even the basest motives have brought men under the preaching, but when Jesus has been lifted up, they have been savingly drawn to Him, and as a consequence have smitten upon their breasts in repentance, and gone their way to serve the Saviour whom they once blasphemed.

Oh, the power, the melting, conquering, transforming power of that dear cross of Christ! My brethren, we have but to abide by the preaching of it, we have but constantly to tell abroad the matchless story, and we may expect to see the most remarkable spiritual results. We need despair of no man now that Jesus has died for sinners. With such a hammer as the doctrine of the cross, the most flinty heart will be broken; and with such a fire as the sweet love of Christ, the most mighty iceberg will be melted. We need never despair for the heathenish or superstitious races of men; if we can but find occasion to bring the doctrine of Christ crucified into contact with their natures, it will yet change them, and Christ will be their king.

We shall now draw nearer to the text, and in the first place, *analyse the general mourning around the cross;* secondly, we shall, if God shall help us, *endeavour to join in the sorrowful chorus;* and then, ere we conclude, we shall *remind you that at the foot of the cross our sorrow must be mingled with joy.*

I. First, then, let us ANALYSE THE GENERAL MOURNING which this text describes.

"All the people that came together to that sight, beholding the things which were done, smote their breasts, and returned." They all smote their breasts, but not all from the same cause. They were all afraid, not all from the same reason. The outward manifestations were alike in the whole mass, but the grades of difference in feeling were as many as the minds in which they ruled. There were many, no doubt, who were merely moved with a transient emotion. They had seen the death agonies of a remarkable Man, and the attendant wonders had persuaded

D

them that He was something more than an ordinary being, and therefore, they were afraid. With a kind of indefinite fear, grounded upon no very intelligent reasoning, they were alarmed, because God was angry, and had closed the eye of day upon them, and made the rocks to rend; and, burdened with this indistinct fear, they went their way trembling and humbled to their several homes; but peradventure, ere the next morning light had dawned, they had forgotten it all, and the next day found them greedy for another bloody spectacle, and ready to nail another Christ to the cross, if there had been such another to be found in the land.

Their beating of the breast was not a breaking of the heart. It was an April shower, a dewdrop of the morning, a hoar-frost that dissolved when the sun had risen. Like a shadow the emotion crossed their minds, and like a shadow it left no trace behind. How often in the preaching of the cross has this been the only result in tens of thousands! In this house, where so many souls have been converted, many more have shed tears which have been wiped away, and the reason of their tears has been forgotten. A handkerchief has dried up their emotions. Alas! alas! alas! that while it may be difficult to move men with the story of the cross to weeping, it is even more difficult to make those emotions permanent.

"I have seen something wonderful, this morning," said one who had listened to a faithful and earnest preacher, "I have seen a whole congregation in tears." "Alas!" said the preacher, "there is something more wonderful still, for the most of them will go their way to forget that they ever shed a tear." Ah, my hearers, shall it be always so—always so? Then, O ye impenitent, there shall come to your eyes a tear which shall drip for ever, a scalding drop which no mercy shall ever wipe away; a thirst that shall never be abated; a worm that shall never die, and a fire that never shall be quenched. By the love you bear your souls, I pray you escape from the wrath to come!

Others amongst that great crowd exhibited emotion based upon more thoughtful reflection. They saw that they had shared in the murder of an innocent person. "Alas!" said they, "we see through it all now. That Man was no offender. In all that we have ever heard or seen of Him, He did good, and only good: He always healed the sick, fed the hungry, and raised the dead. There is not a word of all His teaching that is really contrary to the law of God. He was a pure and holy Man. We have all been duped. Those priests have egged us on to put to death one whom it were a thousand mercies if we could restore to life again at once. Our race has killed its benefactor." "Yes," saith one, "I thrust out my tongue, I found it almost impossible to restrain myself, when everybody else was laughing and mocking at His tortures; but I am afraid I have mocked at the innocent, and I tremble lest the darkness which ,God has sent was His reprobation of my wickedness in oppressing the innocent."

Such feelings would abide, but I can suppose that they might not bring men to sincere repentance; for while they might feel sorry that they had oppressed the innocent, yet, perceiving nothing more in Jesus than mere maltreated virtue and suffering manhood, the natural emotion might soon pass away, and the moral and spiritual result be of no great value.

How frequently have we seen in our hearers that same description of emotion! They have regretted that Christ should be put to death, they have felt like that old king of France, who said, "I wish I had been there with ten thousand of my soldiers, I would have cut their throats sooner than they should have touched Him"; but those very feelings have been evidence that they did not feel their share in the guilt as they ought to have done, and that to them the cross of Jesus was no more a saving spectacle than the death of a common martyr. Dear hearers, beware of making the cross to be a common-place thing with you. Look beyond the sufferings of the innocent manhood of Jesus, and see upon the tree the atoning sacrifice of Christ, or else you look to the cross in vain.

In the motley company who all went home smiting on their breasts, let us hope that there were some who said, "Certainly this was the Son of God," and mourned to think He should have suffered for their transgressions, and been put to grief for their iniquities. Those who came to that point were saved. Blessed were the eyes that looked upon the slaughtered Lamb in such a way as that, and happy were the hearts that there and then were broken because He was bruised and put to grief for their sakes. Beloved, aspire to this. May God's grace bring you to see in Jesus Christ no other than God made flesh, hanging upon the tree in agony, to die, the just for the unjust, that we may be saved. O come and repose your trust in Him, and then smite upon your breasts at the thought that such a victim should have been necessary for your redemption; then may you cease to smite your breasts, and begin to clap your hands for very joy; for they who thus bewail a Saviour may rejoice in Him, for He is theirs and they are His.

II. We shall now ask you TO JOIN IN THE LAMENTATION, each man according to his sincerity of heart, beholding the cross, and smiting upon his breast.

We will by faith put ourselves at the foot of the little knoll of Calvary: there we see in the centre, between two thieves, the

Son of God made flesh, nailed by His hands and feet, and dying in an anguish which words cannot portray. Look ye well, I pray you; look steadfastly and devoutly, gazing through your tears. 'Tis He who was worshipped of angels, who is now dying for the sons of men; sit down and watch the death of death's destroyer. I shall ask you first to smite your breasts, as you remember that *you see in Him your own sins.* How great He is! That thorn-covered head was once crowned with all the royalties of heaven and earth. He who dies there is no common man. King of kings and Lord of lords is He who hangs on yonder cross.

Then see the greatness of your sins, which required so vast a sacrifice. They must be infinite sins to require an infinite Person to lay down His life in order to obtain their removal. Thou canst never compass or comprehend the greatness of thy Lord in His essential character and dignity, neither shalt thou ever be able to understand the blackness and heinousness of the sin which demanded His life as an atonement. Brother, smite thy breast and say, "God be merciful to me, the greatest of sinners, for I am such." Look well into the face of Jesus, and see how vile they have made Him! They have stained those cheeks with spittle, they have lashed those shoulders with a felon's scourge; they have put Him to the death which was only awarded to the meanest Roman slave; they have hung Him up between heaven and earth, as though He were fit for neither; they have stripped Him naked and left Him not a rag to cover Him!

See here then, O believer, the shame of thy sins. What a shameful thing thy sin must have been; what a disgraceful and abominable thing, if Christ must be made such a shame for thee! O be ashamed of thyself, to think thy Lord should thus be scorned and made nothing of for thee! See how they aggravate His sorrows! It was not enough to crucify Him, they must insult Him; nor that enough, they must mock His prayers and turn His dying cries into themes for jest, while they offer Him vinegar to drink. See, beloved, how aggravating were your sins and mine! Come, my brother, let us both smite upon our breasts and say, "Oh, how our sins have piled up their guiltiness! It was not merely that we broke the law, but we sinned against light and knowledge; against rebukes and warnings. As His griefs are aggravated, even so are our sins!" Look still into His dear face, and see the lines of anguish which indicate the deeper inward sorrow which far transcends mere bodily pain and smart. God, His Father, has forsaken Him. God has made Him a curse for us.

Then what must the curse of God have been against us? What must our sins have deserved? If when sin was only imputed to Christ, and laid upon Him for awhile, His Father turned His head away and made His Son cry out, "Lama Sabachthani!" Oh, what an accursed thing our sin must be, and what a curse would have come upon us; what thunderbolts, what coals of fire, what indignation, and wrath from the most High must have been our portion had not Jesus interposed! If Jehovah did not spare His Son, how little would He have spared guilty, worthless men if He had dealt with us after our sins, and rewarded us according to our iniquities!

As we still sit down and look at Jesus, we remember that His death was voluntary—He need not have died unless He had so willed: here then is another striking feature of our sin, for our sin was voluntary too. We did not sin as of compulsion, but we deliberately chose the evil way. O sinner, let both of us sit down together, and tell the Lord that we have no justification, or extenuation, or excuse to offer, we have sinned wilfully against light and knowledge, against love and mercy. Let us smite upon our breasts, as we see Jesus willingly suffer, and confess that we have willingly offended against the just and righteous laws of a most good and gracious God. I could fain keep you looking into those five wounds, and studying that marred face, and counting every purple drop that flowed from hands and feet, and side, but time would fail us. Only that one wound—let it abide with you—smite your breast because you see in Christ your sin.

Looking again—changing, as it were, our stand-point, but still keeping our eye upon that same, dear crucified One, let us see there *the neglected and despised remedy for our sin.* If sin itself, in its first condition, as rebellion, bring no tears to our eyes, it certainly ought in its second manifestation, as ingratitude. The sin of rebellion is vile; but the sin of slighting the Saviour is viler still. He that hangs on the tree, in groans and griefs unutterable, is He whom some of you have never thought of, whom you do not love, to whom you never pray, in whom you place no confidence, and whom you never serve. I will not accuse you; I will ask those dear wounds to do it, sweetly and tenderly. I will rather accuse myself; for, alas! alas! there was a time when I heard of Him as with a deaf ear; when I was told of Him, and understood the love He bore to sinners, and yet my heart was like a stone within me, and would not be moved. I stopped my ear and would not be charmed, even with such a master-fascination as the disinterested love of Jesus. I think if I had been spared to live the life of an ungodly man, for thirty, forty, or fifty years, and had been converted at last, I should never have been able to blame myself sufficiently for rejecting Jesus during all those years.

Why, even those of us who were converted in our youth, and almost in our childhood, cannot help blaming ourselves to think that so dear a Friend, who had done so much for us, was so long slighted by us. Who could have done more for us than He, since He gave Himself for our sins? Ah, how did we wrong Him while we withheld our hearts from Him! O ye sinners, how can ye keep the doors of your hearts shut against the Friend of Sinners? How can we close the door against Him who cries, "My head is wet with dew, and my locks with the drops of the night: open to me, my beloved, open to me"? I am persuaded there are some here who are His elect: you were chosen by Him from before the foundation of the world, and you shall be with Him in heaven one day to sing His praises, and yet, at this moment, though you hear His name, you do not love Him, and, though you are told of what He did, you do not trust Him. What! shall that iron bar always fast close the gate of your heart? Shall that door still be always bolted? O Spirit of the living God, win an entrance for the blessed Christ this morning! If anything can do it, surely it must be a sight of the crucified Christ; that matchless spectacle shall make a heart of stone relent and melt, by Jesus' love subdued. O may the Holy Ghost work this gracious melting, and He shall have all the honour.

Still keeping you at the cross foot, dear friends, every believer here may well smite upon his breast this morning as he thinks of *who it was that smarted so upon the cross.* Who was it? It was He who loved us or ever the world was made. It was He who is this day the Bridegroom of our souls, our Best-beloved; He who has taken us into the banqueting house and waved His banner of love over us; He who has made us one with Himself, and has vowed to present us to His Father without spot. It is He, our Husband, our Ishi, who has called us His Hephzibah because His soul delighteth in us. It is He who suffereth thus for us.

Suffering does not always excite the same degree of pity. You must know something of the individual before the innermost depths of the soul are stirred; and so it happens to us that the higher the character and the more able we are to appreciate it, the closer the relation and the more fondly we reciprocate the love, the more deeply does suffering strike the soul. You are coming to His table some of you to-day, and you will partake of bread: I pray you remember that it represents the quivering flesh that was filled with pain on Calvary. You will sip of that cup: then be sure to remember that it betokens to you the blood of One who loves you better than you could be loved by mother, or by husband, or by friend. O sit you down and smite your breasts that He should grieve; that heaven's Sun should be eclipsed; that heaven's Lily should be spotted with blood, and heaven's Rose should be whitened, with a deadly pallor. Lament that perfection should be accused, innocence smitten, and love murdered; and that Christ, the happy and the holy, the ever blessed, who had been for ages the delight of angels, should now become the sorrowful, the acquaintance of grief, the bleeding and the dying. Smite upon your breasts, believers, and go your way!

Beloved in the Lord, if such grief as this should be kindled in you, it will be well to pursue the subject, and to reflect upon how unbelieving and how cruel we have been to Jesus since the day that we have known Him. What, doth He bleed for me and have I doubted Him? Is He the Son of God, and have I suspected His fidelity? Have I stood at the cross foot unmoved? Have I spoken of my dying Lord in a cold, indifferent spirit? Have I ever preached Christ crucified with a dry eye and a heart unmoved? Do I bow my knee in private prayer, and are my thoughts wandering when they ought to be bound hand and foot to His dear bleeding self? Am I accustomed to turn over the pages of the Evangelists which record my Master's wondrous sacrifice, and have I never stained those pages with my tears? Have I never paused spell-bound over the sacred sentence which recorded this miracle of miracles, this marvel of marvels? Oh, shame upon thee, hard heart! Well may I smite thee. May God smite thee with the hammer of His Spirit, and break thee to shivers. O thou stony heart, thou granite soul, thou flinty spirit, well may I strike the breast which harbours thee, to think that I should be so doltish in presence of love so amazing, so divine.

Brethren, you may smite upon your breasts as you look at the cross, and mourn that you should have done so little for your Lord. I think if anybody could have sketched my future life in the day of my conversion, and have said, "You will be dull and cold in spiritual things! and you will exhibit but little earnestness and little gratitude!" I should have said like Hazael, "Is thy servant a dog, that he should do this great thing?" I suppose I read your hearts when I say that the most of you are disappointed with your own conduct as compared with your too-flattering prophecies of yourselves!

What! am I really pardoned? Am I in very deed washed in that warm stream which gushed from the riven side of Jesus, and yet am I not wholly consecrated to Christ? What! in my body do I bear the marks of the Lord Jesus, and can I live almost without a thought of Him? Am I plucked like a brand from the burning, and have I small care to win others from the wrath to come? Has Jesus stooped to win me, and do I not labour to win others for Him? Was He all in earnest about me, and am I only half in earnest about him? Dare I waste a minute, dare I trifle away an hour? Have I an evening to spend in vain gossip and idle frivolities?

O my heart, well may I smite thee, that at the sight of the death of the dear Lover of my soul, I should not be fired by the highest zeal, and be impelled by the most ardent love to a perfect consecration of every power of my nature, every affection of my spirit, every faculty of my whole man? This mournful strain might be pursued to far greater lengths. We might follow up our confessions, still smiting, still accusing, still regretting, still bewailing. We might continue upon the bass notes evermore, and yet might we not express sufficient contrition for the shameful manner in which we have treated our blessed Friend. We might say with one of our hymn writers—

> "Lord, let me weep for nought but sin,
> And after none but Thee;
> And then I would—O that I might—
> A constant weeper be!"

III. Let me invite you, in the third place, to remember that AT CALVARY, DOLOROUS NOTES ARE NOT THE ONLY SUITABLE MUSIC.

We admired our poet when, in the hymn which we have just sung, he appears to question with himself which would be the most fitting tune for Golgotha.

> " 'It is finished'; shall we raise
> Songs of sorrow or of praise?
> Mourn to see the Saviour die,
> Or proclaim His victory?
>
> If of Calvary we tell,
> How can songs of triumph swell?
> If of man redeemed from woe,
> How shall notes of mourning flow?"

He shows that since our sin pierced the side of Jesus, there is cause for unlimited lamentation, but since the blood which flowed from the wound has cleansed our sin, there is ground for unbounded thanksgiving; and therefore, the poet, after having balanced the matter in a few verses, concludes with—

> " 'It is finished,' let us raise
> Songs of thankfulness and praise."

After all, you and I are not in the same condition as the multitude who had surrounded Calvary; for at that time our Lord was still dead, but now He is risen indeed. There were yet three days from that Thursday evening (for there is much reason to believe that our Lord was not crucified on Friday), in which Jesus must dwell in the regions of the dead. Our Lord, therefore, so far as human eyes could see Him, was a proper object of pity and mourning, and not of thanksgiving; but now, beloved,

He ever lives and gloriously reigns. No charnal house confines that blessed body. He saw no corruption; for the moment when the third day dawned, He could no longer be held with the bond of death, but He manifested Himself alive unto His disciples. He tarried in this world for forty days. Some of His time was spent with those who knew Him in the flesh; perhaps a larger part of it was passed with those saints who came out of their graves, after His resurrection; but certain it is that He is gone up, as the first-fruit from the dead; He is gone up to the right hand of God, even the Father. Do not bewail those wounds, they are lustrous with supernal splendour. Do not lament His death: He lives no more to die. Do not mourn that shame and spitting—

> "The head that once was crowned with thorns,
> Is crowned with glory now."

Look up and thank God that death hath no more dominion over Him. He ever liveth to make intercession for us, and He shall shortly come with angelic bands surrounding Him, to judge the quick and dead. The argument for joy overshadows the reason for sorrow. Like as a woman when the man-child is born remembereth no more her anguish, for joy that a man is born into the world, so, in the thought of the risen Saviour, who has taken possession of His crown, we will forget the lamentation of the cross, and the sorrows of the broken heart of Calvary.

Moreover, hear ye the shrill voice of the high sounding cymbals, and let your hearts rejoice within you, for in His death our Redeemer conquered all the hosts of hell. They came against Him furiously, yea, they came against Him to eat up his flesh, but they stumbled and fell. They compassed Him about, yea, they compassed Him about like bees; but in the name of the Lord did the Champion destroy them. Against the whole multitude of sins, and all the battalions of the pit, the Saviour stood, a solitary soldier fighting against innumerable bands, but He has slain them all. "Bruised is the dragon's head." Jesus has led captivity captive. He conquered when He fell; and let the notes of victory drown for ever the cries of sorrow.

Moreover, brethren, let it be remembered that men have been saved. Let there stream before your gladdened eyes this morning the innumerable company of the elect. Robed in white they come in long procession; they come from distant lands, from every clime; once scarlet with sin and black with iniquity, they are all white and pure, and without spot before the throne for ever; beyond temptation, beatified, and made life to Jesus. And how? It was all through Calvary. There was their sin put away; there was their everlasting righteousness brought in and consummated. Let the hosts that are before the throne, as they wave their palms, and touch their golden harps, excite you to a joy like their own, and let that celestial music hush the gentler voices which mournfully exclaim—

> "Alas! and did my Saviour bleed?
> And did my Sovereign die?
> Would He devote that sacred head
> For such a worm as I?"

Nor is that all. You yourself are saved. O brother, this will always be one of your greatest joys. That others are converted through your instrumentality is occasion for much thanksgiving, but your Saviour's advice to you is, "Notwithstanding in this rejoice not, that the spirits are subject unto you; but rather rejoice, because your names are written in heaven." You, a spirit meet to be cast away, you whose portion must have been with devils—*you* are this day forgiven, adopted, saved, on the road to heaven. Oh! while you think that you are saved from hell, that you are lifted up to glory, you cannot but rejoice that your sin is put away from you through the death of Jesus Christ, your Lord.

Lastly, there is one thing for which we ought always to remember Christ's death with joy, and that is, that although the crucifixion of Jesus was intended to be a blow at the honour and glory of our God—though in the death of Christ the world did, so far as it was able, put God Himself to death, and so earn for itself that hideous title, "a decidal world," yet never did God have such honour and glory as He obtained through the suffering of Jesus. Oh, they thought to scorn Him, but they lifted His Name on high! They thought that God was dishonoured when He was most glorified. The image of the Invisible, had they not marred it? The express image of the Father's person, had they not defiled it? Ah, so they said! But He that sitteth in the heavens may well laugh and have them in derision, for what did they? They did but break the alabaster box, and all the blessed drops of infinite mercy streamed forth to perfume all worlds. They did but rend the veil, and then the glory which had been hidden between the cherubim shone forth upon all lands. O nature, adoring God with thine ancient and priestly mountains, extolling him with thy trees, which clap their hands, and worshipping with thy seas, which in their fulness roar out Jehovah's praise; with all thy tempests and flames of fire, thy dragons and thy deeps, thy snow and thy hail, thou canst not glorify God as Jesus glorified Him when He became obedient unto death. O heaven, with all thy jubilant angels, thine ever chanting cherubim and seraphim, thy thrice holy hymns, thy streets of gold and endless harmonies, thou canst not reveal the Deity as Jesus Christ revealed it on the cross. O hell, with all thine infinite horrors and flames unquenchable, and pains and griefs and shrieks of tortured ghosts, even thou canst not reveal the justice of God as Christ revealed it in His riven heart upon the bloody tree. O earth and heaven and hell! O time and eternity, things present and things to come, visible and invisible, ye are dim mirrors of the Godhead compared with the bleeding Lamb. O heart of God, I see Thee nowhere as at Golgotha, where the Word incarnate reveals the justice and the love, the holiness and the tenderness of God in one blaze of glory. If any created mind would fain see the glory of God, he need not gaze upon the starry skies, nor soar into the heaven of heavens, he has but to bow at the cross foot and watch the crimson streams which gush from Immanuel's wounds.

If you would behold the glory of God, you need not gaze between the gates of pearls, you have but to look beyond the gates of Jerusalem and see the Prince of Peace expire. If you would receive the noblest conception that ever filled the human mind of the loving kindness and the greatness and the pity, and yet the justice and the severity and the wrath of God, you need not lift up your eyes, nor cast them down, nor look to paradise, nor gaze on Tophet, you have but to look into the heart of Christ all crushed and broken and bruised, and you have seen it all. Oh, the joy that springs from the fact that God has triumphed after all! Death is not the victor; evil is not master. There are not two rival kingdoms, one governed by the God of good, and the other by the God of evil; no, evil is bound, chained, and led captive; its sinews are cut, its head is broken; its king is bound to the dread chariot of Jehovah-Jesus, and as the white horses of triumph drag the Conqueror up the everlasting hills in splendour of glory, the monsters of the pit cringe at His chariot wheels. Wherefore, beloved, we close this discourse with this sentence of humble yet joyful worship, "Glory be unto the Father, and to the Son, and to the Holy Ghost: as it was in the beginning is now and ever shall be, world without end. Amen."

CHRIST MADE A CURSE FOR US

A SERMON

Text.—"Christ hath redeemed us from the curse of the law, being made a curse for us: for it is written, Cursed is every one that hangeth on a tree."—Galatians iii. 13.

THE apostle had been showing to the Galatians that salvation is in no degree by works. He proved this all-important truth in the verses which precede the text, by a very conclusive form of double reasoning. He showed, first, that the law could not give the blessing of salvation, for, since all had broken it, all that the law could do was to curse. He quotes the substance of the twenty-seventh chapter of Deuteronomy, "Cursed is every one that continueth not in all things which are written in the book of the law to do them"; and as no man can claim that he has continued in all things that are in the law, he pointed out the clear inference that all men under the law had incurred the curse.

He then reminds the Galatians, in the second place, that if any had ever been blessed in the olden times, the blessing came not by the law, but by their faith, and to prove this, he quotes a passage from Habakkuk ii. 4, in which it is distinctly stated, that the just shall live by faith: so that those who were just and righteous, did not live before God on the footing of their obedience to the law, but they were justified and made to live on the ground of their being believers. See, then, that if the law inevitably curses us all, and if the only people who are said to have been preserved in gracious life were justified not by works, but by faith, then is it certain beyond a doubt that the salvation and justification of a sinner cannot be by the works of the law, but altogether by the grace of God through faith which is in Christ Jesus.

But the apostle, no doubt feeling that now he was declaring that doctrine, he had better declare the foundation and root of it, unveils in the text before us a reason why men are not saved by their personal righteousness, but saved by their faith. He tells us that the reason is this: that men are not saved now by any personal merit, but their salvation lies in another—lies, in fact, in Christ Jesus, the representative Man, who alone can deliver us from the curse which the law brought upon us; and since works do not connect us with Christ, but faith is the uniting bond, faith becomes the way of salvation. Since faith is the hand that lays hold upon the finished work of Christ, which works could not and would not do for works lead us to boast and to forget Christ, faith becomes the true and only way of obtaining justification and everlasting life.

In order that such faith may be nurtured in us, may God the Holy Spirit this morning lead us into the depths of the great work of Christ; may we understand more clearly the nature of His substitution, and of the suffering which it entailed upon Him. Let us see, indeed, the truth of the stanzas whose music has just died away—

> "He bore that we might never bear
> His Father's righteous ire."

I. Our first contemplation, this morning, will be upon this question, WHAT IS THE CURSE OF THE LAW HERE INTENDED?

It is the curse of God. God who made the law has appended certain penal consequences to the breaking of it, and the man who violates the law, becomes at once the subject of the wrath of the Lawgiver. It is not the curse of the mere law of itself; it is a curse from the great Lawgiver whose arm is strong to defend His statutes. Hence, at the very outset of our reflections, let us be assured that the law-curse must be supremely just, and morally unavoidable. It is not possible that our God, Who delights to bless us, should inflict an atom of curse upon any one of His creatures unless the highest right shall require it; and if there be any method by which holiness and purity can be maintained without a curse, rest assured the God of love will not imprecate sorrow upon His creatures.

The curse then, if it fall, must be a necessary one, in its very essence needful for the preservation of order in the universe, and for the manifestations of the holiness of the universal Sovereign. Be assured, too, that when God curses, it is a curse of the most weighty kind. The curse causeless shall not come; but God's curses are never causeless, and they come home to offenders with overwhelming power. Sin must be punished, and when by long continuance and impenitence in evil, God is provoked to speak the malediction, I wot that he whom He curses, is cursed indeed. There is something so terrible in the very idea of the omnipotent God pronouncing a curse upon a transgressor, that my blood curdles at it, and I cannot express myself very clearly or even coherently.

A father's curse, how terrible! but what is that to the malediction of the great Father of Spirits! To be cursed of men is no mean evil, but to be accursed of God is terror and dismay.

Sorrow and anguish lie in that curse; death is involved in it and that second death which John foresaw in Patmos, and described as being cast into a lake of fire. Rev. xx. 14. Hear ye the word of the Lord by his servant Nahum, and consider what His curse must be: "God is jealous, and the Lord revengeth; the Lord revengeth, and is furious; the Lord will take vengeance on his adversaries, and he reserveth wrath for his enemies. . . . The mountains quake at him, and the hills melt, and the earth is burned at his presence, yea, the world, and all that dwell herein. Who can stand before his indignation? and who can abide in the fierceness of his anger? his fury is poured out like fire, and the rocks are thrown down by him."

Remember also the prophecy of Malachi: "For behold, the day cometh, that shall burn as an oven; and all the proud, yea, and all that do wickedly, shall be stubble: and the day that cometh shall burn them up, saith the Lord of hosts, that it shall leave them neither root nor branch." Let such words, and there are many like them, sink into your hearts, that ye may fear and tremble before this just and holy Lord.

If we would look further into the meaning of the curse that arises from the breach of the law, we must remember that a curse is first of all a sign of displeasure. Now, we learn from Scripture that God is angry with the wicked every day; though towards the persons of sinners God exhibits great longsuffering, yet sin exceedingly provokes His holy mind; sin is a thing so utterly loathsome and detestable to the purity of the Most High, that no thought of evil, nor an ill word, nor an unjust action, is tolerated by Him; He observes every sin, and His holy soul is stirred thereby. He is of purer eyes than to behold iniquity; He cannot endure it. He is a God that will certainly execute vengeance upon every evil work.

A curse implies something more than mere anger. It is suggested by burning indignation; and truly our God is not only somewhat angry with sinners, but His wrath is great towards sin. Wherever sin exists, there the fulness of the power of the divine indignation is directed; and though the effect of that wrath may be for awhile restrained through abundant long-suffering, yet God is greatly indignant with the iniquities of men. We wink at sin, yes, and even harden our hearts till we laugh at it and take pleasure in it, but oh! let us not think that God is such as we are; let us not suppose that sin can be beheld by Him and yet no indignation be felt. Ah! no, the most holy God has written warnings in His word which plainly inform us how terribly He is provoked by iniquity, as, for instance, when He saith, "Beware, ye that forget God, lest I tear you in pieces, and there be none to deliver." "Therefore saith the

Lord, the Lord of hosts, the mighty One of Israel, Ah, I will ease me of mine adversaries, and avenge me of mine enemies.'' "For we know him that hath said, Vengeance belongeth unto me, I will recompense, saith the Lord. And again, the Lord shall judge his people. It is a fearful thing to fall into the hands of the living God.''

Moreover, a curse imprecates evil, and is, as it comes from God, of the nature of a threat. It is as though God should say, "By-and-by I will visit thee for this offence. Thou hast broken my law which is just and holy, and the inevitable penalty shall certainly come upon thee.'' Now, God has throughout His word given many such curses as these: He has threatened men over and over again. "If he turn not, he will whet his sword; he hath bent his bow, and made it ready.'' Sometimes the threatening is wrapped up in a plaintive lamentation. "Turn ye, turn ye from your evil ways; for why will ye die, O house of Israel?''

But still it is plain and clear that God will not suffer sin to go unpunished, and when the fulness of time shall come, and the measure shall be filled to the brim, and the weight of iniquity shall be fully reached, and the harvest shall be ripe, and the cry of wickedness shall come up mightily into the ears of the Lord God of Sabaoth, then will He come forth in robes of vengeance and overwhelm His adversaries.

But God's curse is something more than a threatening; He comes at length to blows. He uses warning words at first, but sooner or later He bares His sword for execution. The curse of God, as to its actual infliction, may be guessed at by some occasions wherein it has been seen on earth. Look at Cain, a wanderer and a vagabond upon the face of the earth! Read the curse that Jeremiah pronounced by the command of God upon Pashur; "Behold, I will make thee a terror to thyself, and to all thy friends: and they shall fall by the sword of their enemies, and thine eyes shall behold it.''

Or, if you would behold the curse upon a larger scale, remember the day when the huge floodgates of earth's deepest fountains were unloosed, and the waters leaped up from their habitations like lions eager for their prey. Remember the day of vengeance when the windows of heaven were opened, and the great deep above the firmament was confused with the deep that is beneath the firmament, and all flesh were swept away, save only the few who were hidden in the ark which God's covenant mercy had prepared—when sea-monsters whelped and stabled in the palaces of ancient kings, when millions of sinners sank to rise no more, when universal ruin flew with raven wing over a shoreless sea vomited from the mouth of death. Then was the curse of God poured out upon the earth.

Look ye yet again further down in time. Stand with Abraham at his tent door, and see towards the east the sky all red at early morning with a glare that came not from the sun; sheets of flames went up to heaven, which were met by showers of yet more vivid fire, which preternaturally descended from the skies. Sodom and Gomorrah, having given themselves up to strange flesh, received the curse of God, and hell was rained upon them out of heaven until they were utterly consumed.

If you would see another form of the curse of God, remember that bright spirit who once stood as servitor in heaven, the son of the morning, one of the chief of the angels of God. Think how he lost his lofty principality when sin entered into him! See how an archangel became an archfiend, and Satan, who is called Apollyon, fell from his lofty throne, banished for ever from peace and happiness, to wander through dry places, seeking rest and finding none, to be reserved in chains of darkness unto the judgment of the last great day. Such was the curse that it withered an angel into a devil, it burned up the cities of the plain, it swept away the population of a globe.

Nor have you yet the full idea. There is a place of woe and horror, a land of darkness as darkness itself, and of the shadow of death, without any order, and there the light is darkness. There those miserable spirits who have refused repentance, and have hardened themselves against the Most High, are for ever banished from their God and from all hope of peace or restoration. The curse of God is to lose God's favour; consequently, to lose the blessings which come upon that favour; to lose peace of mind, to lose hope, ultimately to lose life itself; for "the soul that sinneth, it shall die"; and that loss of life, and being cast into eternal death, is the most terrible of all, consisting as it does in everlasting separation from God and everything that makes existence truly life. A destruction lasting on for ever, according to the scriptural description of it, is the fruit of the curse of the law.

Oh, heavy tidings have I to deliver this day to some of you! Hard is my task to have to testify to you thus the terrible justice of the law. But you would not understand or prize the exceeding love of Christ if you heard not the curse from which He delivers His people, therefore hear me patiently. O unhappy men, unhappy men, who are under God's curse to-day! You may dress yourselves in scarlet and fine linen, you may go to your feasts, and drain your full bowls of wine; you may lift high the sparkling cup, and whirl in the joyous dance, but if God's curse be on you, what madness possesses you! O sirs, if you could but see it, and understand it, this curse would darken all the windows of your mirth. Let us fly to the dear cross of

Christ, where the curse was put away, that we may never come to know in the fulness of its horror what the curse may mean.

II. A second enquiry of great importance to us this morning is this: WHO ARE UNDER THIS CURSE?

Listen with solemn awe, O sons of men. First, especially and foremost, the Jewish nation lies under the curse, for such I gather from the connection. To them the law of God was very peculiarly given beyond all others. They heard it from Sinai, and it was to them surrounded with a golden setting of ceremonial symbol, and enforced by solemn national covenant. Moreover, there was a word in the commencement of that law which showed that in a certain sense it peculiarly belonged to Israel. "I am the Lord thy God, which brought thee out of the land of Egypt, from the house of bondage." Paul tells us that those who have sinned without law shall be punished without law; but the Jewish nation, having received the law, if they broke it, would become peculiarly liable to the curse which was threatened for such breach.

Yet further, all nations that dwell upon the face of the earth are also subject to this curse, for this reason: that if the law was not given to all from Sinai, it has been written by the finger of God more or less legibly upon the conscience of all mankind. It needs no prophet to tell an Indian, a Laplander, a South Sea Islander, that he must not steal; his own judgment so instructs him. There is that within every man which ought to convince him that idolatry is folly, that adultery and unchastity are villainies, that theft, and murder, and covetousness, are all evil.

Now, inasmuch as all men in some degree have the law within, to that degree they are under the law; the curse of the law of transgression comes upon them. Moreover, there are some in this house this morning who are peculiarly under the curse. The apostle says, "As many as are of the works of the law are under the curse." Now, there are some of you who choose to be under the law; you deliberately choose to be judged by it. How so? Why, you are trying to reach a place in heaven by your own good works; you are clinging to the idea that something you can do can save you; you have therefore elected to be under the law, and by so doing you have chosen the curse, for all that the law of works can do for you, is to leave you still accursed, because you have not fulfilled all its commands. O sirs, repent of so foolish a choice, and declare henceforth that you are willing to be saved by grace, and not at all by the works of the law. Thou art under the curse as thou now art, but I rejoice to have to tell thee that the curse has been removed through Jesus Christ our Lord. O may the Lord lead thee to see the plan of substitution and to rejoice in it.

E

III. Our third and main point, this morning, is to answer the question, HOW WAS CHRIST MADE A CURSE FOR US?

The whole pith and marrow of the religion of Christianity lies in the doctrine of "substitution," and I hesitate not to affirm my conviction that a very large proportion of Christians are not Christians at all, for they do not understand the fundamental doctrine of the Christian creed; and alas! there are preachers who do not preach, or even believe this cardinal truth. They speak of the blood of Jesus in an indistinct kind of way, and descant upon the death of Christ in a hazy style of poetry, but they do not strike this nail on the head, and lay it down that the way of salvation is by Christ's becoming a substitute for guilty man.

This shall make me the more plain and definite. Sin is an accursed thing. God, from the necessity of His holiness, must curse it; He must punish men for committing it; but the Lord's Christ, the glorious Son of the everlasting Father, became a Man, and suffered in His own proper person the curse which was due to the sons of men, that so, by a vicarious offering, God having been just in punishing sin, could extend His bounteous mercy towards those who believe in the Substitute. Now for this point. But, you enquire, how was Jesus Christ a curse?

We beg you to observe the word "made." "He was *made* a curse." Christ was no curse in Himself. In His person He was spotlessly innocent, and nothing of sin could belong personally to Him. In Him was no sin. "God made him to be sin for us," the apostle expressly adds, "who knew no sin." There must never be supposed to be any degree of blameworthiness or censure in the person or character of Christ as He stands as an individual. He is in that respect without spot or wrinkle, or any such thing, the immaculate Lamb of God's Passover. Nor was Christ made a curse of necessity. There was no necessity in Himself that He should ever suffer the curse; no necessity except that which His own loving suretyship created. His own intrinsic holiness kept Him from sin, and that same holiness kept Him from the curse. He was made a sin *for us*, not on His own account, not with any view to Himself, but wholly because He loved us, and chose to put Himself in the place which we ought to have occupied. He was made a curse for us not, again I say, out of any personal desert, or out of any personal necessity, but because He had voluntarily undertaken to be the covenant head of His people, and to be their representative, and as their representative to bear the curse which was due to them.

Let us go farther into this truth. How was Christ made a curse? In the first place, He was made a curse because all the sins of His people were actually laid on Him. Remember the words of the apostle—it is no doctrine of mine, mark you; it is an inspired sentence, it is God's doctrine—"He made him to be sin for us;" and let me quote another passage from the prophet Isaiah, "The Lord hath laid on him the iniquity of us all;" and yet another from the same prophet, "He shall bear their iniquities." The sins of God's people were lifted from off them and imputed to Christ, and their sins were looked upon as if Christ had committed them. He was regarded as if He had been the sinner; He actually and in very deed stood in the sinner's place. Next to the imputation of sin came the curse of sin. The law, looking for sin to punish, with its quick eye detected sin laid upon Christ, and, as it must curse sin wherever it was found, it cursed the sin as it was laid on Christ.

So Christ was made a curse. Wonderful and awful words but as they are scriptural words, we must receive them. Sin being on Christ, the curse came on Christ, and in consequence, our Lord felt an unutterable horror of soul. Surely it was that horror which made Him sweat great drops of blood when He saw and felt that God was beginning to treat Him as if He had been a sinner. The holy soul of Christ shrunk with deepest agony from the slightest contact with sin. So pure and perfect was our Lord, that never an evil thought had crossed His mind, nor had His soul been stained by the glances of evil, and yet He stood in God's sight a sinner and therefore a solemn horror fell upon His soul; the heart refused its healthful action, and a bloody sweat bedewed His face. Then He began to be made a curse for us, nor did He cease till He had suffered all the penalty which was due on our account.

We have been accustomed in divinity to divide the penalty into two parts, the penalty of loss and the penalty of actual suffering. Christ endured both of these. It was due to sinners that they should lose God's favour and presence, and therefore Jesus cried, "My God, my God, why hast thou forsaken me?" It was due to sinners that they should lose all personal comfort; Christ was deprived of every consolation, and even the last rag of clothing was torn from Him, and He was left like Adam naked and forlorn. It was necessary that the soul should lose everything that could sustain it, and so did Christ lose every comfortable thing; He looked and there was no man to pity or help; He was made to cry, "But I am a worm, and no man; a reproach of men, and despised of the people."

As for the second part of the punishment, namely, an actual infliction of suffering, our Lord endured this also to the uttermost, as the evangelists clearly show. You have read full often the story of His bodily sufferings; take care that you never depreciate them. There was an amount of physical pain endured

by our Saviour which His body never could have borne unless
it had been sustained and strengthened by union with His Godhead; yet the sufferings of His soul were the soul of His sufferings.
That soul of His endured a torment equivalent to hell itself.
The punishment that was due to the wicked was that of hell,
and though Christ suffered not hell, He suffered an equivalent
for it; and now, can your minds conceive what that must have
been?

It was an anguish never to be measured, an agony never to
be comprehended. It is to God, and God alone that His griefs
were fully known. Well does the Greek liturgy put it, "Thine
unknown sufferings," for they must for ever remain beyond
guess of human imagination. See, brethren, Christ has gone
thus far; He has taken the sin, taken the curse, and suffered
all the penalty. The last penalty of sin was death; and therefore the Redeemer died. Behold, the mighty conqueror yields
up His life upon the tree! His side is pierced; the blood and
water flows forth, and His disciples lay His body in the tomb.
As He was first numbered with the transgressors, He was afterwards numbered with the dead. See, beloved, here is Christ
bearing the curse instead of His people. Here He is coming
under the load of their sin, and God does not spare Him but
smites him, as He must have smitten us, lays His full vengeance
on Him, launches all His thunderbolts against Him, bids the
curse wreak itself upon Him, and Christ suffers all, sustains all.

IV. And now let us conclude by considering WHAT ARE THE
BLESSED CONSEQUENCES OF CHRIST'S HAVING THUS BEEN MADE A
CURSE FOR US.

The consequences are that He hath redeemed us from the
curse of the law. As many as Christ died for, are for ever free
from the curse of the law; for when the law cometh to curse a
man who believeth in Christ, he saith, "What have I to do with
thee, O law? Thou sayest, 'I will curse thee,' but I reply,
'Thou hast cursed Christ instead of me. Canst thou curse twice
for one offence?'" Behold how the law is silenced! God's law
having received all it can demand, is not so unrighteous as to
demand anything more. All that God can demand of a believing sinner, Christ has already paid, and there is no voice in earth
or heaven that can henceforth accuse a soul that believes in
Jesus.

You were in debt, but a friend paid your debt; no writ can
be served on you. It matters nothing that *you* did not pay it,
it is paid, and you have the receipt. That is sufficient in any
court of equity. So with all the penalty that was due to us,
Christ has borne it. It is true I have not borne it; I have not
been to hell and suffered the full wrath of God, but Christ has

suffered that wrath for me, and I am as clear as if I had myself paid the debt to God and had myself suffered His wrath.

Here is a glorious bottom to rest upon! Here is a rock upon which to lay the foundation of eternal comfort! Let a man once get to this. My Lord without the city's gate did bleed for me as my Surety, and on the cross discharged my debt. Why, then, great God, Thy thunders I no longer fear. How canst Thou smite me now? Thou hast exhausted the quiver of Thy wrath; every arrow has been already shot forth against the person of my Lord, and I am in Him clear and clean, and absolved and delivered, even as if I had never sinned. "He hath redeemed us," saith the text.

How often I have heard certain gentry of the modern school of theology sneer at the atonement, because they charge us with the notion of its being a sort of business transaction, or what they choose to call "the mercantile view of it." I hesitate not to say that the mercantile metaphor expresses rightly God's view of redemption, for we find it so in Scripture; the atonement is a ransom—that is to say, a price paid; and in the present case the original word is more than usually expressive; it is a payment for, a price instead of. Jesus did in His sufferings perform what may be forcibly and fitly described as the payment of a ransom, the giving to justice a *quid pro quo* for what was due on our behalf for our sins. Christ in His person suffered what we ought to have suffered in our persons. The sins that were ours were made His; He stood as a sinner in God's sight; though not a sinner in Himself, He was punished as a sinner, and died as a sinner upon the tree of the curse.

Then having exhausted His imputed sinnership by bearing the full penalty, He made an end of sin, and He rose again from the dead to bring in that everlasting righteousness which at this moment covers the persons of all His elect, so that they can exultingly cry, "Who shall lay anything to the charge of God's elect? It is God that justifieth. Who is he that condemneth? It is Christ that died, yea, rather, that is risen again, who is even at the right hand of God, who also maketh intercession for us."

Another blessing flows from this satisfactory substitution. It is this, that now the blessing of God, which had been hitherto arrested by the curse is made most freely to flow. Read the verse that follows the text: "That the blessing of Abraham might come on the Gentiles through Jesus Christ; that we might receive the promise of the Spirit through faith." The blessing of Abraham was that in his seed all nations of the earth should be blessed. Since our Lord Jesus Christ has taken away the curse due to sin, a great rock has been lifted out from the river-bed of God's mercy, and the living stream comes rippling, rolling, swelling on in crystal tides, sweeping before it all human sin and sorrow, and making glad the thirsty who stoop down to drink thereat.

O my brethren, the blessings of God's grace are full and free this morning; they are as full as your necessities. Great sinners, there is great mercy for you. They are as free as your poverty could desire them to be, free as the air you breathe, or as the cooling stream that flows along the water-brook. You have but to trust Christ, and you shall live. Be you who you may, or what you may, or where you may, though at hell's dark door you lie down to despair and die, yet the message comes to you, "God hath made Christ to be a propitiation for sin. He made him to be sin for us who knew no sin, that we might be made the righteousness of God in him."

Christ hath delivered us from the curse of the law, being made a curse for us. He that believeth, hath no curse upon him. He may have been an adulterer, a swearer, a drunkard, a murderer, but the moment he believes, God sees none of those sins in him. He sees him as an innocent man, and regards his sins has having been laid on the Redeemer, and punished in Jesus as He died on the tree. I tell thee, if thou believest in Christ this morning, my hearer, though thou be the most damnable of wretches that ever polluted the earth, yet thou shalt not have a sin remaining on thee after believing. God will look at thee as pure; even Omniscience shall not detect a sin in thee, for thy sin shall be put on the scapegoat, even Christ, and carried away into forgetfulness, so that if thy transgression be searched for, it shall not be found. If thou believest—there is the question —thou art clean; if thou wilt trust the incarnate God, thou art delivered. He that believeth is justified from all things. "Believe on the Lord Jesus Christ, and thou shalt be saved," for "he that believeth and is baptised, shall be saved; and he that believeth not shall be damned."

I have preached to you the gospel, God knows with what a weight upon my soul, and yet with what holy joy. This is no subject for gaudy eloquence, and for high-flying attempts at oratory; this is a matter to be put to you plainly and simply. Sinners—you must either be cursed of God, or else you must accept Christ, as bearing the curse instead of you. I do beseech you, as you love your souls, if you have any sanity left, accept this blessed and divinely-appointed way of salvation. This is the truth which the apostles preached, and suffered and died to maintain; it is this for which the Reformers struggled; it is this for which the martyrs burned at Smithfield; it is the grand basis doctrine of the Reformation, and the very truth of God.

CHRIST MADE A CURSE FOR US

Down with your crosses and rituals, down with your pretensions to good works, and your crouchings at the feet of priests to ask absolution from them! Away with your accursed and idolatrous dependence upon yourself; Christ has finished salvation-work, altogether finished it. Hold not up your rags in competition with His fair white linen: Christ has borne the curse; bring not your pitiful penances, and your tears all full of filth to mingle with the precious fountain flowing with His blood. Lay down what is your own, and come and take what is Christ's. Put away now everything that you have thought of being or doing, by way of winning acceptance with God; humble yourselves, and take Jesus Christ to be the Alpha and Omega, the first and last, the beginning and end of your salvation.

If you do this, not only shall you be saved, but you are saved: rest, thou weary one, for thy sins are forgiven; rise, thou lame man, lame through want of faith, for thy transgression is covered; rise from the dead, thou corrupt one, rise, like Lazarus from the tomb, for Jesus calleth thee! Believe and live. The words in themselves, by the Holy Spirit, are soul-quickening. Have done with thy tears of repentance and thy vows of good living, until thou hast come to Christ; then take them up as thou wilt. Thy first lesson should be none but Jesus, none but Jesus, none but Jesus. O come thou to Him! See, He hangs upon the cross; His arms are open wide, and He cannot close them, for the nails hold them fast. He tarries for thee; His feet are fastened to the wood, as though He meant to tarry still. O come thou to Him! His heart has room for thee. It streams with blood and water; it was pierced for thee. That mingled stream is—

> "Of sin the double cure,
> To cleanse *thee* from its guilt and power."

An act of faith will bring thee to Jesus. Say, "Lord, I believe, help thou mine unbelief;" and if thou so doest, He cannot cast thee out, for His word is, "Him that cometh to me I will in no wise cast out." I have delivered to you the weightiest truth that ever ears heard, or that lips spoke, put it not from you. As we shall meet each other at the last tremendous day, when heaven and earth are on a blaze, and the trumpet shall ring and raise the dead, as we shall meet each other then, I challenge you to put this from you. If you do it, it is at your own peril, and your blood be on your own heads; but the rather accept the gospel I have delivered to you. It is Jehovah's gospel. Heaven itself speaks in the words you hear to-day. Accept Jesus Christ as your substitute. O do it now, this moment, and God shall have glory, but you shall have salvation. Amen.

"BOUGHT WITH A PRICE"

A Sermon

Text.—"Ye are not your own: for ye are bought with a price: therefore glorify God in your body, and in your spirit, which are God's."—1 Cor. vi. 19, 20.

You will notice that in this chapter the apostle Paul has been dealing with sins of the flesh, with fornication and adultery. Now, it is at all times exceedingly difficult for the preacher either to speak or to write upon this subject; it demands the strictest care to keep the language guarded, so that while we are denouncing a detestable evil we do not ourselves promote it by a single expression that should be otherwise than chaste and pure. Observe how well the apostle Paul succeeds, for though he does not mask the sin, but tears the veil from it, and lets us know well what it is that he is aiming at, yet there is no sentence which we could wish to alter. Herein he is a model for all ministers, both in fidelity and prudence.

Be sure also to note that the apostle, when he is exposing sin, does not trifle with it, but like a mighty hunter before the Lord, pursues it with all his might; his hatred to it is intense; he drags it forth to the light; he bids us mark its hideous deformity; he hunts it through all its purlieus, hotfoot, as we say. He never leaves it breathing time: argument after argument he hurls like javelins upon it; he will by no means spare the filthy thing. He who above all others speaks most positively of salvation by grace, and is most clear upon the fact that salvation is not by the works of the law, is at the same time most intensely earnest for the holiness of Christians, and most zealously denounces those who would say, "Let us do evil, that good may come."

In this particular instance he sets the sin of fornication in the light of the Holy Spirit; he holds up, as it were, the seven-branched candlestick before it, and lets us see what a filthy thing it is. He tells us that the body is the temple of the Holy Ghost, and therefore ought not to be profaned; he declares that bodily unchastity is a sacrilegious desecration of our manhood, a violation of the sacred shrine wherein the Spirit takes up its dwelling-place; and then, as if this were not enough, he seizes the sin and drags it to the foot of the cross, and there nails it hand and foot, that it may die as a criminal; for these are his

68

words: "Ye are not your own: for ye are bought with a price:" the price being the blood of Jesus. He finds no sharper weapon, no keener instrument of destruction than this. The redemption wrought on Calvary by the death of Jesus must be the death of this sin, and of all other sins, wherever the Spirit of God uses it as his sword of execution.

Brethren and sisters, it is no slight thing to be holy. A man must not say, "I have faith," and then fall into the sins of an unbeliever; for, after all, our outer life is the test of our inner life; and if the outer life be not purified, rest assured the heart is not changed. That faith which does not bring forth the fruit of holiness is the faith of devils. The devils believe and tremble. Let us never be content with a faith which can live in hell, but rise to that which will save us—the faith of God's elect, which purifies the soul, casting down the power of evil, and setting up the throne of Jesus Christ, the throne of holiness within the spirit.

Noticing this as being the run of the chapter, we now come to the text itself, and in order to discuss it we must take it to pieces, and I think we shall see in it at once three things very clearly. The first is *a blessed fact*, "Ye are," or as it should be rendered, "Ye were bought with a price;" then comes a *plain consequence* from that fact, a consequence of a double character, negative and positive: "Ye are not your own;" "your body and your spirit are God's;" and out of that there springs inevitably *a natural conclusion:* "Therefore, glorify God in your body, and in your spirit."

I. Let us begin, then, first of all, with this BLESSED FACT— "*Ye are bought with a price.*" Paul might, if his object were to prove that we are not our own, have said: "Ye did not make yourselves." Creation may well furnish motives for obedience to the great Lawgiver. He might also have said, "Ye do not preserve yourselves: it is God who keeps you in life; you would die if He withdrew His power." The preservation of divine providence might furnish abundant arguments for holiness. Surely He who feeds, nourishes, and upholds our life should have our service. But He prefers, for reasons known to Himself, which it would not be hard to guess, to plead the tenderer theme, redemption. He sounds that note, which if it do not thunder with that crash of power which marked the six days' labour of Omnipotence, yet has a soft, piercing, subduing tone in it, which, like the still small voice to which Elias listened, has in it the presence of God.

The most potent plea for sanctity is not "Ye were made," or, "Ye are nourished," but "Ye are bought." This the apostle selects as a convincing proof of our duty, and as a means to make that duty our delight. And truly, beloved, it is so. If we have indeed experienced the power of redemption we fully admit that it is so. Look ye back to the day when ye were bought, when ye were bondslaves to your sins, when ye were under the just sentence of divine justice, when it was inevitable that God should punish your transgressions; remember how the Son of God became your substitute, how He bared his back to the lash that should have fallen upon you, and laid His soul beneath the sword which should have quenched its fury in your blood. You were redeemed then, redeemed from the punishment that was due to you, redeemed from the wrath of God, redeemed unto Christ to be His for ever.

You will notice the text says, "Ye were bought *with a price.*" It is a common classical expression to signify that the purchase was expensive. Of course, the very expression, "Ye were bought," implies a price, but the words "*with a price*" are added, as if to show that it was not for nothing that ye were purchased. There was a something inestimably precious paid for you; and ye need scarcely that I remind you that "ye were not redeemed with corruptible things, as silver and gold;" "but with the precious blood of Christ, as of a lamb without blemish and without spot."

Ah! those words slip over our tongue very glibly, but we may well chide ourselves that we can speak of redemption with dry eyes. That the blood of Christ was shed to buy our souls from death and hell is a wonder of compassion which fills angels with amazement, and it ought to overwhelm us with adoring love whenever we think of it, glance our eye over the recording pages, or even utter the word "redemption."

What meant this purchasing us *with blood?* It signified pain. Have any of you lately been racked with pain? Have you suffered acutely? Ah! then at such times you know to some degree what the price was which the Saviour paid. His bodily pains were great, hands and feet nailed to the wood, and the iron breaking through the tenderest nerves. His soul-pains were greater still, His heart was melted like wax, He was very heavy, His heart was broken with reproach, He was deserted of God, and left beneath the black thunder-clouds of divine wrath, His soul was exceeding sorrowful, even unto death. It was pain that bought you. We speak of the drops of blood, but we must not confine our thoughts to the crimson life-floods which distilled from the Saviour's veins; we must think of the pangs which He endured, which were the equivalent for what we ought to have suffered, what we must have suffered had we endured the punishment of our guilt for ever in the flames of hell.

But pain alone could not have redeemed us; it was by death that the Saviour paid the ransom. Death is a word of horror to the ungodly. The righteous hath hope in His death; but as

Christ's death was the substitute for the death of the ungodly, He was made a curse for us, and the presence of God was denied Him. His death was attended with unusual darkness; He cried, "My God, my God, why hast thou forsaken me?" O think ye earnestly on this. The Ever-living died to redeem us; the Only Begotten bowed His head in agony, and was laid in the grave that we might be saved. Ye are bought then "with a price"— a price incalculable, stupendous, infinite, and this is the plea which the apostle uses to urge upon us that we should "be holiness to the Lord." Holiness, therefore, is necessary to all the redeemed. If you cast off your responsibility to be holy, you at the same time cast away the benefit of redemption. Will you do this? As I am sure you could not renounce your salvation, and cast away your only hope, so I charge you by the living God be not so inconsistent as to say: "I am redeemed, and yet I will live as I list." As redeemed men, let the inevitable consequences follow from the fact, and be ye evidently the servants of the Lord Jesus.

Remember, too, that *this fact is the most important one in all your history.* That you were redeemed "with a price" is the greatest event in your biography. Oh, I do beseech you then, if it be so, prove it; and remember the just and righteous proof is by your not being your own, but consecrated unto God. If it be the most important thing in the world to you, that you were "bought with a price," let it exercise the most prominent influence over your entire career. Be a man, be an Englishman, but be most of all Christ's man. A citizen, a friend, a philanthropist, a patriot: all these you may be, but be most of all a saint redeemed by blood.

Recollect, again, that your being "bought with a price" *will be the most important fact in all your future existence.* What say they in heaven when they sing? They would naturally select the noblest topic and that which most engrosses their minds, and yet in the whole range of their memory they find no theme so absorbing as this: "Thou wast slain, and hast redeemed us to God by thy blood." Redeeming love is the theme of heaven. When you reach the upper realms your most important memory will not be that you were wealthy or poor in this life, nor the fact that you sickened and died, but that you were "bought with a price."

We do not know all that may occur in this world before the close of its history; but certainly it will be burnt up with fire and you in yonder clouds with Christ may witness the awful conflagration. You will never forget it. There will be new heavens and new earth, and you with Christ may see the new-born heavens and earth, laughing in the bright sunlight of God's good pleasure; you will never forget that joyous day. And you

will be caught up to dwell with Jesus for ever and ever; and there
will come a time when He shall deliver up the kingdom to God,
even the Father, and God shall be all in all. You will never forget the time of which the poet sings—

> "Then the end, beneath His rod
> Man's last enemy shall fall.
> Hallelujah, Christ in God,
> God in Christ is all in all."

All these divinely glorious events will impress themselves upon
you, but not one of them will make an impression so lasting, so
clear, so deep as this, that you were "bought with a price." High
over all the mountain tops, Calvary, that was but a little mount
in human estimation, shall rise; stars shall the events of history
be; but this event shall be the sun in whose presence all others
hide their diminished heads. "Thou wast slain," the full chorus
of heaven shall roll it forth in thundering accents of grateful
zeal. "Thou wast slain, and hast redeemed us to God by thy
blood"; the saints shall remember this first and foremost; and
amidst the cycles of eternity this shall have the chief place in every
glorified memory. What then, beloved? Shall it not have the
chief place with you now? It has been *the fact* of your life hitherto,
it will be the fact of your entire eternal existence: let it saturate
your soul, let it penetrate your spirit, let it subdue your faculties,
let it take the reins of all your powers and guide you whither it
will; let the Redeemer, He whose hands were pierced for you,
sway the sceptre of your spirit and rule over you this day, and
world without end.

If I had the power to do it, how would I seek to refresh in your
souls a sense of this fact that you are "bought with a price?"
There, in the midnight hour, amidst the olives of Gethsemane,
kneels Immanuel the Son of God; He groans, He pleads in prayer,
He wrestles; see the beady drops stand on His brow, drops of
sweat, but not of such sweat as pours from men when they earn
the bread of life, but the sweat of Him who is procuring life
itself for us. It is blood, it is crimson blood; great gouts of it
are falling to the ground. O soul, thy Saviour speaks to thee
from out Gethsemane at this hour, and He says: "Here and thus
I bought thee with a price." Come, stand and view Him in the
agony of the olive garden, and understand at what a cost He
procured thy deliverance. Track Him in all His path of shame
and sorrow till you see Him on the Pavement; mark how they
bind His hands and fasten him to the whipping-post; see, they
bring the scourges and the cruel Roman whips; they tear His
flesh; the ploughers make deep furrows on His blessed body,
and the blood gushes forth in streams, while rivulets from His

temples, where the crown of thorns has pierced them, join to swell the purple stream. From beneath the scourges He speaks to you with accents soft and low, and He says, "My child, it is here and thus I bought thee with a price."

But see Him on the cross itself when the consummation of all has come; His hands and feet are fountains of blood; his soul is full of anguish even to heartbreak; and there, ere the soldier pierces with a spear His side, bowing down He whispers to thee and to me "It was here, and thus, I bought thee with a price"? Oh, by Gethsemane, by Gabbatha, by Golgotha, by every sacred name connected with the passion of our Lord, by sponge and vinegar, and nail and spear, and everything that helped the pang and increased the anguish of His death, I conjure you, my beloved brethren, to remember that ye were "bought with a price," and "are not your own."

I push you to this; you either were or were not so bought; if you were, it is the grand fact of your life; if you were, it is the greatest fact that ever will occur to you: let it operate upon you, let it dominate your entire nature, let it govern your body, your soul, your spirit, and from this day let it be said of you not only that you are a man, a man of good morals and respectable conduct, but this, above all things, that you are a man filled with love to Him who bought you, a man who lives for Christ, and knows no other passion. Would God that redemption would become the paramount influence, the lord of our soul, and dictator of our being; then were we indeed true to our obligations: short of this we are not what love and justice both demand.

II. Now, let us pass on to the second point. Here is A PLAIN CONSEQUENCE arising from the blessed fact. Ye were "bought with a price." Then first it is clear as a *negative*, that "Ye are not your own"; and secondly, it is clear as a *positive*, that "your body and spirit are God's."

Take first *the negative:* if bought, you are not your own. No argument is needed for this, and indeed it is so great a boon in itself that none of us could find it in our hearts to demur to it. It is a great privilege not to be one's own. A vessel is drifting on the Atlantic hither and thither, and its end no man knoweth. It is derelict, deserted by all its crew; it is the property of no man; it is the prey of every storm, and the sport of every wind: rocks, quicksands, and shoals wait to destroy it; the ocean yearns to engulf it. It drifts onward to no man's land, and no man will mourn its shipwreck. But mark well yonder barque in the Thames which its owner surveys with pleasure. In its attempt to reach the sea, it may run ashore, or come into collision with other vessels; or in a thousand ways suffer damage; but there is no fear, it will pass through the floating forest of "the Pool";

it will thread the winding channel, and reach the Nore because its owner will secure it pilotage, skilful and apt.

How thankful you and I should be that we are not derelict to-day! we are not our own, not left on the wild waste of chance to be tossed to and fro by fortuitous circumstances; but there is a hand upon our helm; we have on board a pilot who owns us, and will surely steer us into the Fair Havens of eternal rest. The sheep is on the mountain side, and the winter is coming on; it may be buried in the snow; perhaps the wolf may seize it, or by-and-by, when the summer crops have been eaten, there may be little fodder for it, and it may starve; but the sheep's comfort, if it could think at all, would be this: it is not its own, it belongeth to the shepherd, who will not willingly lose his property; it bears the mark of its owner, and is the object of his care. O happy sheep of God's pasture, what a bliss it is to you that you are not your own! Does any man here think it would be a pleasure to be his own? Let me assure him that there is no ruler so tyrannical as self. He that is his own master, has a fool and a tyrant to be his lord. No man ever yet governed himself after the will of the flesh, but what he by degrees found the yoke heavy and the burden crushing. Self is a fierce dictator, a terrible oppressor; imperious lusts are cruel slave-drivers.

But Christ, who says we are not our own, would have us view that truth in the light in which a loving wife would view it. She, too, is not her own. She gave herself away on a right memorable day, of which she bears the golden token on her finger. She did not weep when she surrendered herself and became her husband's; nor did they muffle the bells, or bid the organ play the "Dead March" in Saul: it was a happy day for her; she remembers it at this moment with glowing joy. She is not her own, but she has not regretted the giving herself away: she would make the same surrender again to the self-same beloved owner, if it were to be done. That she is her husband's does not bespeak her slavery, but her happiness; she has found rest in her husband's house, and to-day, when the Christian confesses that he is not his own, he does not wish that he were. He is married to the Saviour; he has given himself up, body, soul, and spirit, to the blessed Bridegroom of his heart; it was the marriage-day of his true life when he became a Christian, and he looks back to it with joy and transport. Oh, it is a blissful thing not to be our own, so I shall not want arguments to prove that to which every gracious spirit gives a blissful consent.

Now, if it be true that we are not our own, and I hope it is true to many here present, then the inference from it is, "I have no right to *injure myself* in any way." My body is not my own, I have no right then, as a Christian man, to do anything with it that would defile it. The apostle is mainly arguing against sins of the flesh, and he says, "the body is not for fornication, but for the Lord; and the Lord for the body." We have no right to commit uncleanness, because our bodies are the members of Christ and not our own. He would say the same of drunkenness, gluttony, idle sleep, and even of such excessive anxiety after wealth as injures health with carking care. We have no right to profane or injure the flesh and blood which are consecrated to God; every limb of our frame belongs to God; it is His property; He has bought it "with a price." Any honest man will be more concerned about an injury done to another's property placed under his care, than if it were his own.

When the son of the prophet was hewing wood with Elisha, you remember how he said, when the axe head flew off into the water, "Alas! master, for it was borrowed." It would be bad enough to lose my own axe, but it is not my own, therefore I doubly deplore the accident. I know this would not operate upon thievish minds. There are some who, if it was another man's, and they had borrowed it, would have no further care about it: "Let the lender get it back, if he can." But we speak to honest men, and with them it is always a strong argument: Your body is another's, do it no injury. As for our spirit too, that is God's, and how careful we should be of it.

I am asked sometimes to read an heretical book: well, if I believed my reading it would help its refutation, and might be an assistance to others in keeping them out of error, I might do it as a hard matter of duty, but I shall not do it unless I see some good will come from it. I am not going to drag my spirit through a ditch for the sake of having it washed afterwards, for it is not my own. It may be that good medicine would restore me if I poisoned myself with putrid meat, and I am not going to try it: I dare not experiment on a mind which no longer belongs to me. There is a mother and a child, and the child has a book to play with, and a blacklead pencil. It is making drawings and marks upon the book, and the mother takes no notice. It lays down one book and snatches another from the table, and at once the mother rises from her seat, and hurriedly takes the book away, saying: "No, my dear, you must not mark that, for it is not ours."

So with my mind, intellect, and spirit; if it belonged to me I might or might not play tomfool with it, and go to hear Socinians, Ritualists, Universalists, and such like preach, but as it is not my own, I will preserve it from such fooleries, and the pure word shall not be mingled with the errors of men. Here is the drift of the apostle's argument—I have no right to injure that which does not belong to me, and as I am not my own, I have no right to injure myself.

But, further, I have no right to let myself *lie waste.* The man who had a talent, and went and dug in the earth and hid it, had not he a right to do so? Yes, of course, if it was his own talent, and his own napkin. If any of you have money and do not put it out to interest, if it is all your own, nobody complains. But this talent belonged to the man's master, it was only intrusted to him as a steward, and he ought to have not let it rust in the ground.

So I have no right to let my faculties run to waste since they do not belong to me. If I am a Christian I have no right to be idle. I saw the other day men using picks in the road in laying down new gas-pipes; they had been resting, and just as I passed the clock struck one, and the foreman gave a signal. I think he said, "*Blow up*"; and straightway each man took his pick or his shovel, and they were all at it in earnest. Close to them stood a fellow with a pipe in his mouth, who did not join in the work, but stood in a free-and-easy posture. It did not make any difference to him whether it was one o'clock or six. Why not? Because he was his own: the other men were the master's for the time being. He as an independent gentleman might do as he liked, but those who were not their own fell to labour. If any of you idle professors can really prove that you belong to yourselves, I have nothing more to say to you, but if you profess to have a share in the redeeming sacrifice of Christ, I am ashamed of you if you do not go to work the very moment the signal is given. You have no right to waste what Jesus Christ has bought "with a price."

Further than that, if we are not our own, but "are bought with a price," we have no right to exercise any *capricious government* of ourselves. A man who is his own may say, "I shall go whither I will, and do what I will"; but if I am not my own but belong to God who has bought me, then I must submit to His government; His will must be my will, and His directions must be my law. I desire to enter a certain garden, and I ask the gardener at the gate if I may come in. "You should be very welcome, sir, indeed," says he, "if it were mine, but my master has told me not to admit strangers here, and therefore I must refuse you." Sometimes the devil would come into the garden of our souls. We tell him that our flesh might consent, but the garden is not ours, and we cannot give him space. Worldly ambition, covetousness, and so forth, might claim to walk through our soul, but we say, "No, it is not our own; we cannot, therefore, do what our old will would do, but we desire to be obedient to the will of our Father who is in heaven." Thy will be done, my God, in me, for so should it be done where all is Thine own by purchase.

Yet, again, if we are not our own, then we have no right *to serve ourselves.* The man who is living entirely for himself, whose object is his own ease, comfort, honour, or wealth, what knows he concerning redemption by Christ? If our aims rise no higher than our personal advantages, we are false to the fact that we "are bought with a price," we are treacherous to Him in whose redemption we pretend to share.

But time would fail me if I dwelt upon this, or, indeed, at any length upon *the positive side* of this blessed fact: I will therefore only say a word or two concerning it. Our body and our spirit are God's; and, Christian, this is certainly a very high honour to you. Your body will rise again from the dead at the first resurrection, because it is not an ordinary body, it belongs to God: your spirit is distinguished from the souls of other men; it is God's spirit, and He has set His mark upon it, and honoured you in so doing. You are God's because a price has been paid for you. According to some, the allusion price here is to the dowry that was paid by a husband for his wife in ancient days. According to the Rabbis there were three ways by which a woman became the wife of a man, and one of these was by the payment of a dowry. This was always held good in Jewish law; the woman was not her own from the moment when the husband had paid to her father or natural guardian the stipulated price for her. Now, at this day, you and I rejoice that Jesus Christ has espoused us unto Himself in righteousness or ever the earth was; we rejoice in that language which He uses by the prophet Hosea, "I will betroth thee unto me for ever"; but here is our comfort, the dowry money has been paid, Christ has redeemed us unto Himself, and Christ's we are, Christ's for ever and ever.

III. And now I must close, and oh, may God give power to His word while I beg to speak upon the last point, namely, THE NATURAL CONCLUSION, "Therefore glorify God in your body, and in your spirit." I am not clear that the last few words are in the original. A large number of the old manuscripts and versions, and some of the more important of them, finish the verse at the word "body"—"Therefore glorify God in your body." It was the body the apostle was speaking about, and not the spirit, and there is no necessity for the last words: still we will not further raise the question, but take them as being the inspired word of God: but still, I must make the remark, that according to the connection the force of the apostle's language falls upon the body; and perhaps it is so, because we are so apt to forget the truth, that the body is redeemed and is the Lord's, and should be made to glorify God.

The Christian man's body should glorify God by its chastity. Pure as the lily should we be from every taint of uncleanness. The body should glorify God by temperance also; in all things, in eating, drinking, sleeping, in everything that has to do with

F

the flesh. "Whether ye eat or drink, or whatsoever ye do, do all to the glory of God," or as the apostle puts it elsewhere, "whatsoever ye do in word or deed, do all in the name of the Lord Jesus, giving thanks to God and the Father by him." The Christian man can make every meal a sacrament, and his ordinary avocations the exercise of his spiritual priesthood. The body ought to glorify God by its industry. A lazy servant is a bad Christian. A working man who is always looking for Saturday night, a man who never spends a drop of sweat except when the master is looking on, does not glorify God in his body. The best Christian is the man who is not afraid of hard work when it is due, who works not as an eye-servant or man pleaser, but in single-ness of heart seeks to glorify God. Our bodies used to work hard enough for the devil; now they belong to God we will make them work for Him. Your legs used to carry you to the theatre; be not too lazy to come out on a Thursday night to the house of God. Your eyes have been often open upon iniquity, keep them open during the sermon: do not drop asleep! Your ears have been sharp enough to catch the word of a lascivious song, let them be quick to observe the word of God. Those hands have often squandered your earnings in sinfulness, let them give freely to the cause of Christ. Your body was a willing horse when it was in the service of the devil, let it not be a sluggish hack now that it draws the chariot of Christ. Make the tongue speak His praises, make the mouth sing of His glory, make the whole man bow in willing subservience to the will of Him who bought it.

As for your spirit, let that glorify God too. Let your private meditations magnify God; let your songs be to Him when no one hears you but Himself, and let your public zeal, let the purity of your conversation, let the earnestness of your life, let the universal holiness of your character, glorify God with your body and with your spirit.

Beloved Christian friends, I want to say these few things and have done. Because you are God's you will be looked at more than others, therefore, glorify Him. For my part I am very glad of the lynx eyes of the worldlings. Let them watch if they will. I have heard of one who was a great caviller at Christian people, and after having annoyed a church a long time, he was about to leave, and therefore, as a parting jest with the minister, he said, "I have no doubt you will be very glad to know that I am going a hundred miles away?" "No," said the pastor, "I shall be sorry to lose you." "How? I never did you any good." "I don't know that, for I am sure that never one of my flock put half a foot through the hedge but what you began to yelp at him, and so you have been a famous sheep-dog for me." I am glad the world observes us. It has a right to do so. If a man says,

"I am God's," he sets himself up for public observation. Ye are lights in the world, and what are lights intended for but to be looked at? A city set on a hill cannot be hid.

Moreover, the world has a right to expect more from a Christian than from anybody else. He says he is "bought with a price," he says he is God's, he therefore claims more than others, and he ought to render more. If we are not holy and gracious, ungodly men are sure to say, "That is one of your believers in God; that is one of your Chrisitians." Do not let it be so. Every soldier in a regiment ought to feel that the renown of the whole army depends upon him, and he must fight as if the winning of the battle rested upon himself. This will cause every man to be a hero. Oh, that every Christian felt as if the honour of God and the church rested upon him, for in a measure it certainly does!

May we so seek God, that when we come to die we may feel that we have lived for something; that although our hope has rested alone in what Jesus did, yet we have not made that an excuse for doing nothing ourselves. Though we shall have no good works in which to glory, yet may we bring forth fruit that shall be for the glory of our Lord. I feel I so desire to glorify God, body, soul, and spirit while I breathe, that I would even do so on earth after I am dead. I would still urge my brethren on in our Lord's cause.

Old Zizka, the Hussite leader, when about to die, said to his soldiers: "Our enemies have always been afraid of my name in the time of battle, and when I am dead take my skin, and make a drum-head of it, and beat it whenever you go to battle. When the foemen hear the sound they will tremble, and you will remember that Zizka calls on his brethren to fight valiantly." Let us so live that when we die, we live on, like Abel, who being dead yet speaketh. The only way to do this is to live in the power of the Immortal God, under the influence of his Holy Spirit: then out of our graves we shall speak to future generations.

When Doctor Payson died, he desired that his body should be placed in a coffin, and that his hearers should be invited to come and see it. Across his breast was placed a paper bearing these words, "Remember the words which I spoke unto you, being yet present with you." May our lives be such that even if we are not public speakers, yet others may remember our example, and so may hear what our lives spake while we were yet on earth. Your bodies and your spirits are God's: oh, live to God, and glorify Him in the power of His Spirit as long as you have any breath below, that so when the breath is gone, your very bones, like those of Joseph, shall be a testimony. Even in the ashes of the saints their wonted fires live on. In their hallowed memories they rise like a phœnix from their ashes.

The Lord make us more and more practically His own, and may His Name be glorious, for ever and ever. Amen, and amen.

LOVE'S CROWNING DEED

A Sermon

Text.—"Greater love hath no man than this, that a man lay down his life for his friends."—John xv. 13.

I HAVE lately in my ministry very much detained you in the balmy region of divine lovingkindness. Our subjects have frequently been full of love. I have, perhaps, repeated myself, and gone over the same ground again and again, but I could not help it; my own soul was in a grateful condition, and therefore out of the abundance of the heart the mouth hath spoken. Truly I have little reason to excuse myself, for the region of love to Christ is the native place of the Christian; we were first brought to know Christ and to rest in Him through His love, and there, in the warmth of His tenderness, we were born to God. Not by the terrors of justice, nor the threats of vengeance, were we reconciled, but grace drew us with cords of love.

Now, we have sometimes heard of sickly persons, that the physician has recommended them to try their native air, in hopes of restoration; so we also recommend every backsliding Christian to try the native air of Christ's love, and we charge every healthy believer to abide in it. Let the believer go back to the cross again; there he found his hope, there he must find it again: there his love to Jesus began,—we "love him because he first loved us,"—and there must his love be again inflamed.

Our subject this morning, then, is divine love, and we have chosen our highest hill in all the goodly land for you to climb; we shall take you to-day to love's most sacred shrine, to the Jerusalem of the holy land of love, to the Tabor of love, where it was transfigured, and put on its most beautiful garments, where it became indeed too bright for mortal eye fully to gaze upon it, too lustrous for this dim vision of ours. Let us come to Calvary where we find love stronger than death, conquering the grave for our sakes.

We shall speak, first, upon *love's crowning act:* "Greater love hath no man than this, that a man lay down his life for his friends"; but, then, since the text, grand as it is, and high, so that we cannot attain unto it, yet seems to fall short of the great argument, though it be one of the Master's own sayings, we shall

speak upon *the sevenfold crown of Jesus' love;* and when we have
so done, we shall have some *royal things* to say, which befit the
place whereon we stand when we are gathered at the cross-foot.

I. First, then, LOVE'S CROWNING DEED. There is a climax to
everything, and the climax of love is to die for the beloved one.
"Free grace and dying love" are the noblest themes among men,
and when united they are sublimity itself. Love can do much,
can do infinite things, but greater love hath no man than this,
that he lay down his life for his friends. This is the *ultima thule*
of love; its sails can find no further shore, its deeds of self-denial
can go no further. To lay down one's life is the most that love
can do.

This is clear if we consider, first, that when a man dies for his
friends, it proves *his deep sincerity.* Lip-love, proverbially, is a
thing to be questioned; too often is it a counterfeit. Love which
speaks can use hyperbolical expressions at its will, but when you
have heard all you can hear of love's speech, you are not sure
that it is love; for all are not hunters that blow the horn, all are
not friends who cry up friendship. Much there is among men
of a feeling which wears all the likeness of that priceless thing
called love, which is more precious than the gold of Ophir,
and yet for all that, as all is not gold that glitters, so it is not all
love that walketh delicately and feigneth affection.

But a man is no liar when he is willing to die to prove his love.
All suspicion of insincerity must then be banished. We are
sure he loves who dies for love. Yea, it is not bare sincerity that
we see in such a case, we see *the intensity of his affection.* A man
may make us feel that he is intensely in earnest when he speaks
with burning words, and he may perform many actions which
may all appear to show how intense he is, and yet for all that
he may but be a skilful player, understanding well the art of
simulating that which he does not feel: but when a man dies for
the cause he has espoused, you know that his is no superficial
passion, you are sure that the core of his nature must be on fire
when his love consumes his life; if he will shed his blood for the
object beloved, there must be blood in the veins of his love, it
is a living love.

And, again, *it proves the thorough self-abnegation of the heart* when
the man risks life itself for love. Love and self-denial for the
object loved go hand-in-hand. If I profess to love a certain
person, and yet will neither give my silver nor my gold to relieve
his wants, nor in any way deny myself comfort or ease for his
sake, such love is contemptible: it wears the name, but lacks
the reality of love: true love must be measured by the degree
to which the person loving will be willing to subject himself to
crosses and losses, to sufferings and self-denials. After all, the

value of a thing in the market is what a man will give for it, and you must estimate the value of a man's love by that which he is willing to give up for it. What will he do to prove his affection? What will he suffer for the sake of benefitting his beloved? Greater love for friends hath no man than this, that he lay down his life for them.

Even Satan acknowledged the reality of the virtue which would lead a man to die, when he spake concerning Job to God: he made little of Job's losing his sheep, and his cattle, and his children, and remaining patient; but he said, "Skin for skin; ay all that a man hath will he give for his life; but put forth now thine hand, and touch his bone and his flesh, and he will curse thee to thy face." So if love could give up its cattle and its land, its outward treasures and possessions, it would be somewhat strong, but comparatively it would fail if it could not go further, and endure personal suffering, ay, and the laying down of life itself.

No such failure occurred in the Redeemer's love. Our Saviour stripped Himself of all His glories, and by a thousand self-denials proved His love; but the most convincing evidence was given when He gave up His life for us. "Hereby perceive we the love of God," says the apostle John, "because he laid down his life for us"; as if He passed by everything else, which the Son of God had done for us, and put His finger upon His death and said, "*Hereby* we perceive the love of God towards us." It was majestic love that made the Lord Jesus lay aside "his tire and rings of light," and lend their glory to the stars, strip off His azure mantle and hang it on the sky, and then come down to earth to wear the poor, mean garments of our flesh and blood, in which to toil and labour like ourselves; but the master-piece of love was when He would even put off the garment of His flesh, and yield Himself to the agonies superlative of death by crucifixion. He could go no further; self-abnegation had achieved its utmost; He could deny Himself no more, when He denied Himself leave to live.

Again, beloved, the reason why death for its object is the crowning deed of love is this, that *it excels all other deeds*. Jesus Christ had proved His love by dwelling among His people as their Brother, and participating in their poverty as their friend, till He could say, "Foxes have holes and the birds of the air have nests, but I, the Son of Man, have not where to lay my head"; He had manifested His love by telling them all He knew of the Father, unveiling the secrets of eternity to simple fishermen; He showed His love by the patience with which He bore with their faults, never harshly rebuking, but only gently chiding them, and even that but seldom; He revealed His love to them by the miracles He wrought on their behalf, and the honour which He put upon them by using them in His service; indeed, there were ten thousand princely acts of the love of Jesus Christ towards His own, but none of them can for a moment endure comparison with His dying for them,—the agonising death of the cross surpasses all the rest. These life-actions of His love are bright as stars, and, like the stars, if you gaze upon them, they will be seen to be far greater than you dreamed, but yet they are only stars compared with this clear, blazing sun of infinite love which is to be seen in the Lord's dying for His people on the bloody tree.

Then, I must add that His death *did in effect comprehend all other acts*, for when a man lays down his life for his friend he ha s laid down everything else. Give up life, and you have given up wealth—where is the wealth of a dead man? Renounce life, and you have relinquished position—where is the rank of a man who lies in the sepulchre? Lay down life, and you have forsaken enjoyment—what enjoyment can there be to the denizen of the charnel-house? Giving up life, you have given up all things, hence the force of that reasoning, "He that spared not his own Son but freely delivered him up for us all, how will he not with him also freely give us all things?" The giving of the life of His dear Son was the giving of all that His Son was; and as Christ is infinite, and all in all, the delivering up of His life was the concession of all in all to us: there could be nothing more.

Beloved, I speak but too coldly upon a theme which ought to stir my soul first, and yours afterwards. Spirit of the living God, come like a quickening wind from heaven, and let the sparks of our love glow into a mighty furnace-flame just now, even now, if it may so please thee!

Beloved, we now remark that for a man to die for his friends is evidently *the grandest of all proofs of his love in itself*. The words glide over my tongue, and drop from my lips very rapidly—"lay down his life for his friends," but do you know or feel what the words mean? To die for another! There be some who will not even give of their substance to the poor; it seems like wrenching away a limb for them to give a trifle to God's poor servants; such people cannot guess what it must be to have love enough to die for another, any more than a blind man can imagine what colours can be like: such persons are out of court altogether. There have been loving spirits who have denied themselves comfort and ease, and even common necessaries, for the sake of their fellow men, and such as these are in a measure qualified to form an idea of what it must be to die for another; but still none of us can fully know what it means! To die for another!

Conceive it! Concentrate your thoughts upon it! We start back from death, for under any light in which you may place it, human nature can never regard death as otherwise than a terrible thing.

It is no light thing to die. We speak too flippantly of death, but dying is no child's play to any man, and dying as the Saviour died, in awful agonies of body and tortures of soul, it was a great thing indeed for His love to do. You may surround death if you please with luxury, you may place at the bedside all the dear assuagements of the tenderest love; you may alleviate pain by the art of the apothecary and the physician, and you may decorate the dying couch with the honour of a nation's anxious care, but death, for all that, is in itself no slight thing, and when borne for others it is the masterpiece of love.

And so, closing this point of love's crowning action, let me say that *after a man has died for another, there can be no question raised about his love.* Unbelief would be insane if it should venture to intrude itself at the cross-foot, though, alas, it has been there, and has there proved its utter unreasonableness. If a man dies for his friend, he must love him, nobody can question that; and Jesus dying for His people must love them: who shall cast a doubt upon that fact? Shame on any of God's children that they should ever raise questions on a matter so conclusively proven! yet, as if the Lord Jesus knew that even this masterpiece of love might still be intruded upon by unbelief, He rose again from the dead, and rose with His love as fresh as ever in His heart, and went to heaven leading captivity captive, His eyes flashing with the eternal love that brought Him down. He passed through the pearly gates, and rode in triumph up to His Great Father's throne, and though He looked upon His Father with love ineffable and eternal, He gazed upon His people too, for His heart was still theirs. Even at this hour from His throne among the seraphim, where He sits in glory, He looketh down upon His people with pitying love and condescending grace.

> "Now, though He reigns exalted high,
>   His love is still as great;
> Well He remembers Calvary,
>   Nor let His saints forget."

He is all love, and altogether love. "Greater love hath no man than this, that a man lay down his life for his friends."

II. THE SEVEN CROWNS OF JESUS' DYING LOVE are our second point. I hope I shall have your interested attention while I show that above that highest act of human love there is a something in Christ's death for love's sake still more elevated. Men's dying for their friends—this is superlative, but Christ's dying for us is as much above man's superlative as that could be above mere commonplace. Let me show you this in seven points.

The first is this—*Jesus was immortal,* hence the special character of His death. When a man lays down his life for his friend, he does not lay down what he could keep altogether; he could only have kept it for a while, even if he had lived as long as mortals can, till grey hairs are on their head he must at last have yielded to the arrows of death. A substitutionary death for love's sake in ordinary cases would be but a slightly premature payment of that debt of nature which must be paid by all.

But such is not the case with Jesus. Jesus needed not die at all; there was no ground or reason why He should die apart from His laying down His life in the room and place and stead of His friends. Up there in the glory was the Christ of God for ever with the Father, eternal and everlasting; no age passed over His brow; we may say of Him. "Thy locks are bushy and black as the raven, thou hast the dew of thy youth." He came to earth and assumed our nature that He might be capable of death, yet remember, though capable of death, His body need not have died; as it was it never saw corruption, because there was not in it the element of sin which necessitated death and decay. Our Lord Jesus, and none but He, could stand at the brink of the grave and say, "No man taketh my life from me, but I lay it down of myself. I have power to lay it down and I have power to take it again." We poor mortal men have only power to die, but Christ had power to live. Crown Him, then! Set a new crown upon His beloved head! Let other lovers who have died for their friends be crowned with silver, but for Jesus bring forth the golden diadem, and set it upon the head of the Immortal who never needed to have died, and yet became a mortal, yielding Himself to death's pangs without necessity, except the necessity of His mighty love.

Note, next, that in the cases of persons who have yielded up their lives for others they may have entertained, and probably did *entertain the prospect that the supreme penalty would not have been extracted from them.* They hoped that they might yet escape. There is an old story of a pious miner, who was in the pit with an ungodly man at work. They had lighted the fuse, and were about to blast a piece of rock with the powder, and it was necessary that they should both leave the mine before the powder exploded: they both got into the bucket, but the hand above which was to wind them up was not strong enough to draw the two together, and the pious miner, leaping from the bucket, said to his friend, "You are an unconverted man, and if you die your soul will be lost. Get up in the bucket as quickly as you can; as for me, I commit my soul into the hands of God, and if I die I am saved." This lover of his neighbour's soul was spared, for he was found in perfect safety arched over by the fragments which had been blown from the rock: he escaped.

But, remember well that such a thing could not occur in the case of our dear Redeemer. He knew that if He was to give a ransom for our souls He had no loophole for escape. He must surely die. Die He or His people must, there was no other alternative. If we were to escape from the pit through Him, He must perish in the pit Himself; there was no hope for Him, there was no way by which the cup could pass from Him. Men have risked their lives for their friends bravely; perhaps had they been certain that the risk would have ended in death they would have hesitated; Jesus was certain that our salvation involved death to Him, the cup must be drained to the bottom, He must endure the mortal agony; and in all the sufferings of death extreme He must not be spared one jot or tittle; yet deliberately, for our sakes, He espoused death that He might espouse us. I say again, bring forth another diadem! Set a second crown upon that once thorn-crowned head! All hail, Immanuel! Monarch of misery, and Lord of love! Was ever love like Thine! Lift up His praises, all ye sons of song! Exalt Him, all ye heavenly ones! Ay, set His throne higher than the stars, and let Him be extolled above the angels, because with full intent He bowed His head to death. He knew that it behoved Him to suffer, it behoved that He should be made a sacrifice for sin, and yet for the joy that was set before Him He endured the cross, despising the shame.

Note a third grand excellency in the crowning deed of Jesus' love, namely, that *He could have had no motive on that death but one of pure, unmingled love and pity.* You remember when the Russian nobleman was crossing the steppes of that vast country in the snow, the wolves followed the sledge in greedy packs, eager to devour the travellers. The horses were lashed to their utmost speed, but needed not the lash, for they fled for their lives from their howling pursuers. Whatever could stay the eager wolves for a time was thrown to them in vain. A horse was loosed: they pursued it, rent it to pieces, and still followed, like grim death. At last a devoted servant, who had long lived with his master's family, said, "There remains but one hope for you; I will throw myself to the wolves, and then you will have time to escape."

There was great love in this, but doubtless it was mingled with a habit of obedience, a sense of reverence to the head of the household, and probably emotions of gratitude for many obligations which had been received through a long course of years. I do not depreciate the sacrifice, far from it; would that there were more of such a noble spirit among the sons of men! but still you can see a wide difference between that noble sacrifice and the nobler deed of Jesus laying down His life for those who never obliged Him, never served Him, who were infinitely His inferiors, and who could have no claims upon His gratitude. If I had seen the nobleman surrender himself to the wolves to save his servant, and if that servant had in former days tried to be an assassin and had sought his life, and yet the master had given himself up for the undeserving menial, I could see some parallel, but as the case stands there is a wide distinction.

Jesus had no motive in His heart but that He loved us, loved us with all the greatness of His glorious nature, loved us, and therefore for love, pure love, and love alone, He gave Himself up to bleed and die.

> "With all His sufferings full in view,
> And woes to us unknown,
> Forth to the task His spirit flew,
> 'Twas love that urged Him on."

Put the third crown upon His glorious head! Oh angels, bring forth the immortal coronet which has been stored up for ages for Him alone, and let it glitter upon that ever blessed brow!

Fourthly, remember, as I have already begun to hint, that in our Saviour's case *it was not precisely, though it was, in a sense, death for His friends.* Greater love hath no man than this towards his friends that he lay down his life for them; read the text so, and it expresses a great truth: but greater love a man may have than to lay down his life for his friends, namely, if he dies for his enemies. And herein is the greatness of Jesus' love, that though He called us "friends," the friendship was all on His side at the first. He called us friends, but our hearts called Him enemy, for we were opposed to Him. We loved not in return for His love. "We hid as it were our faces from him, he was despised, and we esteemed him not."

Oh the enmity of the human heart to Jesus! There is nothing like it. Of all enmities that have ever come from the pit that is bottomless, the enmity of the heart to the Christ of God is the strangest and most bitter of all; and yet for men polluted and depraved, for men hardened till their hearts are like the nether millstone, for men who could not return and could not reciprocate the love He felt, Jesus Christ gave Himself to die. "Scarcely for a righteous man will one die, yet peradventure for a good (benevolent) man one could even dare to die, but God com-

mendeth his love to us in that while we were yet sinners in due
time Christ died for the ungodly."

> "O love of unexampled kind!
> That leaves all thought so far behind;
> Where length, and breadth, and depth, and height,
> Are lost to my astonished sight."

Bring forth the royal diadem again, I say, and crown our loving
Lord, the Lord of love; for as He is King of kings everywhere
else, so is He King of kings in the region of affection.

I shall not, I hope, weary you when I now observe that there
was another glorious point about Christ's dying for us for *we had
ourselves been the cause of the difficulty which required a death.* There
were two brothers on board a raft once, upon which they had
escaped from a foundering ship. There was not enough of
food, and it was proposed to reduce the number that some at
least might be able to live. So many must die. They cast lots
for life and death. One of the brothers was drawn, and was
doomed to be thrown into the sea. His brother interposed
and said, "You have a wife and children at home; I am single,
and therefore can be better spared, I will die instead of you."
"Nay," said his brother, "not so; why should you? the lot has
fallen upon me"; and they struggled with each other in mutual
arguments of love, till at last the substitute was thrown into the
sea.

Now, there was no ground of difference between those two
brothers whatever; they were friends, and more than friends.
They had not caused the difficulty which required the sacrifice
of one of them, they could not blame one another for forcing
upon them the dreadful alternative; but in our case there would
never have been a need for any one to die if we had not been
the offenders, the wilful offenders; and who was the offended
one, whose injured honour required the death? I speak not
untruthfully if I say it was the Christ that died who was Himself
the offended one. Against God the sin had been committed,
against the majesty of the divine Ruler; and in order to wipe
the stain away from divine justice it was imperative that the
penalty should be exacted and the sinful one should die.

So He who was offended took the place of the offender and died,
that the debt due to His own justice might be paid. It is the
case of the judge bearing the penalty which he feels compelled
to pronounce upon the culprit. Like the old classic story of the
father who on the judgment bench condemns his son to lose
his eyes for an act of adultery, and then puts out one of his own
eyes to save an eye for his son, the judge himself bore a portion
of the penalty. In our case, He who vindicated the honour of

His own law, and bore all the penalty, was the Christ who loved those who had offended His sovereignty, and grieved His holiness. I say again—but where are the lips that shall say it aright? —bring forth, bring forth a new diadem of more than imperial splendour, to crown the Redeemer's blessed head anew, and let all the harps of heaven pour forth the richest music in praise of his supreme love.

Note again that there have been men who have died for others, but they have *never borne the sins of others;* they were willing to take the punishment, but not the guilt. But here, ere Christ must die, it must be written, "He was numbered with the transgressors, and he bore the sin of many." "The Lord hath laid on him the iniquity of us all." "He made him to be sin for us who knew no sin, that we might be made the righteousness of God in him." "He was made a curse for us, as it is written, Cursed is every one that hangeth on a tree." Now, far be it from our hearts to say that Christ was ever less than perfectly holy and spotless, and yet there had to be established a connection between Him and sinners by the way of substitution, which must have been hard for His perfect nature to endure. For Him to be hung up between two felons, for Him to be accused of blasphemy, for Him to be numbered with transgressors, for Him to suffer, the just for the unjust, bearing His Father's wrath as if He had been guilty, this is wonderful, and surpasses all thought! Bring forth the brightest crowns and put them on His head, while we pass on to weave a seventh chaplet for that adorable brow.

For remember, once more, the death of Christ was a proof of love superlative, because in His case *He was denied all the helps and alleviations which in other cases make death to be less than death.* I marvel not that a saint can die joyously; well may his brow be placid, and his eye be bright, for he sees his heavenly Father gazing down upon him, and glory waiting him. Well may his spirit be rapt in joy, even while the death-sweat is on his face, for the angels have come to meet him, and he sees the far-off land, and the gates of pearl growing nearer every hour. But ah, to die upon a cross without a pitying eye upon you, surrounded by a scoffing multitude, and to die there appealing to God, who turns away His face, to die with this as your requiem, "My God, my God, why hast thou forsaken me!" to startle the midnight darkness with an "Eli, Eli, lama sabachthani" of awful anguish such as never had been heard before: this is terrible. The triumph of love in the death of Jesus rises clear above all other heroic arts of self-sacrifice! Blessed Lamb of God, our hearts love Thee, we fall at Thy feet in adoring reverence, and magnify Thee in the silence of our souls.

III. Lastly, and I must be very brief, as my time has fled, MANY ROYAL THINGS OUGHT TO BE SUGGESTED TO US BY THIS ROYAL LOVE.

And first, dear brethren, how this thought of Christ's proving His love by His death ennobles self-denial. I do not know how you feel, but I feel utterly mean when I think of what Christ has done for me. To live a life of comparative ease and enjoyment shames me. To work to weariness seems nothing. After all, what are we doing compared with what He has done? Those who can suffer, who can lay down their lives in mission fields, and bear hardships, and poverty, and persecution for Christ,— my brethren, these are to be envied, they have a portion above their brethren. It makes us feel ashamed to be at home and to possess any comforts when Jesus so denied Himself. I say the thought of the Lord's bleeding love makes us think ourselves mean to be what we are, and makes us nothing in our own sight, while it causes us to honour before God, the self-denial of others, and wish that we had the means of practising it.

And oh, how it prompts us to heroism. When you get to the cross you have left the realm of little men: you have reached the nursery of true chivalry. Does Christ die?—then we feel we could die too. What grand things men have done when they have lived in the love of Christ! That story of the Moravians comes to my mind, and I will repeat it, though you may often have heard it, how in the South of Africa there was, years ago, a place of lepers, into which persons afflicted with leprosy were driven. There was a tract of country surrounded by high walls, from which none could escape. There was only one gate, and he who went in never came out again. Certain Moravians looked over the wall and saw two men: one, whose arms had rotted off with leprosy, was carrying on his back another who had lost his legs, and between the two they were making holes in the ground and planting seeds.

The two Moravians thought, "They are dying of a foul disease by hundreds inside that place, we will go and preach the gospel to them." "But," they said, "if you go in, you can never come out again; there you will die of leprosy too." They went in, and they never did come out till they went home to heaven; they died for others for the love of Jesus. Two others of these holy men went to the West Indian Islands, where there was an estate to which a man could not go to preach the gospel unless he was a slave, and these two men sold themselves for slaves, to work as others worked, that they might tell their fellow slaves the gospel. Oh, if we had that spirit of Jesus among us we should do great things. We want it back, and must have it. The church has lost everything when she has lost her old heroism;

she has lost her power to conquer the world when the love of Christ no longer constrains her.

But mark how the heroic in this case is sweetly tinctured and flavoured with gentleness. The chivalry of the olden times was cruel; it consisted very much in a strong fellow cased in steel going about and knocking others to pieces who did not happen to wear similar suits of steel. Now-a-days we could get a good deal of that courage back, I dare say; but we shall be best without it. We want that blessed chivalry of love in which a man feels, "I would suffer any insult from that man if I could do him good for Christ's sake, and I would be a door-mat to my Lord's temple gate, that all who come by might wipe their feet upon me, if they could honour Christ thereby." The grand heroism of being nothing for Christ's sake, or anything for the church's sake, that is the heroism of the cross; for Christ made Himself of no reputation, and took upon Himself the form of a servant, and being found in fashion as a Man, He became obedient unto death, even the death of the cross. O blessed Spirit, teach us to perform like heroic acts of self-abnegation for Jesus' name's sake!

And, lastly, there seems to my ears to come from the cross, a gentle voice that saith, "Sinner, sinner, guilty sinner, I did all this for thee, what hast thou done for me?" and yet another which saith, "Return unto me! Look unto me and be ye saved, all ye ends of the earth." I wish I knew how to preach to you Christ crucified. I feel ashamed of myself that I cannot do better than I have done. I pray the Lord to set it before you in a far better way than any of my words can. But, oh, guilty sinner, there is life in a look at the Redeemer! Turn now your eyes to Him, and trust Him! Simply by trusting him, you shall find pardon, mercy, eternal life, and heaven. Faith is a look at the Great Substitute. God help you to get that look for Jesus' sake. Amen.

THE CROWN OF THORNS

A Sermon

Text.—"And when they had platted a crown of thorns, they put it upon his head."—Matthew xxvii. 29.

BEFORE we enter the common hall of the soldiers, and gaze upon "the sacred head once wounded," it will be well to consider who and what He was who was thus cruelly put to shame. Forget not the intrinsic excellence of His person; for He is the brightness of the Father's glory, and the express image of His person; He is in Himself God over all, blessed for ever, the eternal Word by Whom all things were made, arid by whom all things consist. Though Heir of all things, the Prince of the kings of the earth, He was despised and rejected of men, "a man of sorrows and acquainted with grief"; His head was scornfully surrounded with thorns for a crown, His body was bedecked with a faded purple robe, a poor reed was put into His hand for a sceptre, and then the ribald soldiery dared to stare into His face, and worry Him with their filthy jests:—

> "The soldiers also spit upon that face
> Which angels did desire to have the grace,
> And prophets once to see, but found no place.
> Was ever grief like Thine?"

Forget not the glory to which He had been accustomed aforetime, for ere He came to earth He had been in the bosom of the Father, adored of cherubim and seraphim, obeyed by every angel, worshipped by every principality and power in the heavenly places; yet here He sits, treated worse than a felon, made the centre of a comedy before He became the victim of a tragedy. They sat Him down in some broken chair, covered Him with an old soldier's cloak, and then insulted Him as a mimic monarch:—

> "They bow their knees to Me, and cry, Hail king:
> Whatever scoffs and scornfulness can bring,
> I am the floor, the sink, where they'd fling.
> Was ever grief like Mine?"

What a descent His love to us compelled Him to make! See how low He fell to lift us from our fall! Do not also fail to remember that at the very time when they were thus mocking Him, He was still the Lord of all, and could have summoned twelve legions of angels to His rescue. There was majesty in His misery; He had laid aside, it is true, the glorious pomp imperial of His Father's courts, and He was now the lowly man of Nazareth, but for all that, had He willed it, one glance of those eyes would have withered up the Roman cohorts; one word from those silent lips would have shaken Pilate's palace from roof to foundation; and had He willed it, the vacillating governor and the malicious crowd would together have gone down alive into the pit, even as Korah, Dathan, and Abiram of old.

Lo, God's own Son, heaven's darling, and earth's prince, sits there and wears the cruel chaplet which wounds both mind and body at once, the mind with insult, and the body with piercing smart. His royal face was marred with "wounds which could not cease to bleed, trickling faint and slow," yet that "noblest brow and dearest" had once been fairer than the children of men, and was even then the countenance of Immanuel, God with us. Remember these things, and you will gaze upon Him with enlightened eyes and tender hearts, and you will be able the more fully to enter into fellowship with Him in His griefs. Remember whence He came, and it will the more astound you that He should have stooped so low. Remember what He was, and it will be the more marvellous that He should become our substitute.

And now let us press into the guard-room, and look at our Saviour wearing His crown of thorns. I will not detain you long with any guesses as to what kind of thorns He wore. According to the Rabbis and the botanists there would seem to have been from twenty to twenty-five different species of thorny plants growing in Palestine; and different writers have, according to their own judgments or fancies, selected one and another of these plants as the peculiar thorns which were used upon this occasion. But why select one thorn out of many? He bore not one grief, but all; any and every thorn will suffice; the very dubiousness as to the peculiar species yields us instruction.

The soldiers may have used pliant boughs of the acacia, or shittim tree, that unrotting wood of which many of the sacred tables and vessels of the sanctuary were made; and, therefore, significantly used if such was the case. It may have been true, as the old writers generally consider, that the plant was the *spina Christi*, for it has many small and sharp spines, and its green leaves would have made a wreath such as those with which generals and emperors were crowned after a battle. But we will leave the matter; it was a crown of thorns which pierced

G

His head, and caused Him suffering as well as shame, and that
suffices us. Our inquiry now is, what do we see when our eyes
behold Jesus Christ crowned with thorns? There are six things
which strike me most, and as I lift the curtain I pray you watch
with me, and may the Holy Spirit pour forth His divine
illumination and light up the scene before our wondering
souls.

I. The first thing which is seen by the most casual observer,
before he looks beneath the surface, is A SORROWFUL SPECTACLE.
Here is the Christ, the generous, loving, tender Christ, treated
with indignity and scorn, here is the Prince of Life and Glory
made an object of derision by a ribald soldiery. Behold to-day
the lily among thorns, purity lifting up itself in the midst of
opposing sin. See here the sacrifice caught in the thicket, and
held fast there, as a victim in our stead to fulfil the ancient type
of the ram held by the bushes, which Abraham slew instead of
Isaac. Three things are to be carefully noted in this spectacle
of sorrow.

Here is Christ's *lowliness and weakness triumphed over* by the
lusty legionaries. When they brought Jesus into the guard-room
they felt that He was entirely in their power, and that His claims
to be a king were so absurd as to be only a theme for contemp-
tuous jest. He was but meanly dressed, for He wore only the
smock frock of a peasant—was He a claimant of the purple?
He held His peace—was He the man to stir a nation to sedition?
He was all wounds and bruises, fresh from the scourger's lash—
was He the hero to inspire an army's enthusiasm and over-
turn old Rome? It seemed rare mirth for them, and as wild
beasts sport with their victims, so did they. Many, I warrant
you, were the jibes and jeers of the Roman soldiery at His expense
and loud was the laughter amid their ranks. Look at His face,
how meek He appears! How different from the haughty coun-
tenances of tyrants! To mock His royal claims seemed but natural
to a rough soldiery. He was gentle as a child, tender as a woman;
His dignity was that of calm quiet endurance, and this was not
a dignity whose force these semi-barbarous men could feel,
therefore did they pour contempt upon Him.

Let us remember that our Lord's weakness was undertaken
for our sakes: for us He became a lamb, for us He laid aside
His glory, and therefore it is the more painful for us to see that
this voluntary humiliation of Himself must be made the object
of so much derision and scorn, though worthy of the utmost
praise. He stoops to save us, and we laugh at Him as He stoops;
He leaves the throne that He may lift us up to it, but while He is
graciously descending, the hoarse laughter of an ungodly world
is His only reward. Ah me! was ever love treated after so unlovely

a sort? Surely the cruelty it received was proportioned to the honour it deserved, so perverse are the sons of men.

> "O head so full of bruises!
> Brow that its lifeblood loses!
> Oh great humility.
> Upon His face are falling
> Indignities most galling;
> He bears them all for me."

It was not merely that they mocked His humility, but *they mocked His claims to be a king.* "Aha," they seemed to say, "is this a king? It must be after some uncouth Jewish fashion, surely, that this poor peasant claims to wear a crown. Is this the Son of David? When will He drive Cæsar and his armies into the sea, and set up a new state, and reign at Rome? This Jew, this peasant, is He to fulfil His nation's dream, and rule over all mankind?" Wonderfully did they ridicule this idea, and we do not wonder that they did, for they could not perceive His true glory.

But, beloved, my point lies here, *He was a King* in the truest and most emphatic sense. If He had not been a king, then He would as an impostor have deserved the scorn, but would not have keenly felt it; but being truly and really a king, every word must have stung His royal soul, and every syllable must have cut to the quick His kingly spirit. When the impostor's claims are exposed and held up to scorn, he himself must well know that he deserves all the contempt he receives, and what can he say? But if the real heir to all the estates of heaven and earth has His claims denied and His person mocked at, then is His heart wounded, and rebuke and reproach fill Him with many sorrows. Is it not sad that the Son of God, the blessed and only Potentate, should have been thus disgraced?

Nor was it merely mockery, but *cruelty added pain to insult.* If they had only intended to mock Him they might have platted a crown of straw, but they meant to pain Him, and therefore they fashioned a crown of thorns. Look ye, I pray you, at His person as He suffers under their hands. They had scourged Him till probably there was no part of His body which was not bleeding beneath their blows except His head, and now that head must be made to suffer too. Alas our whole head was sick, and our whole heart faint, and so He must be made in His chastisement like to us in our transgression. There was no part of our humanity without sin, and there must be no part of His humanity without suffering. If we had escaped in some measure from iniquity, so might He have escaped from pain, but as we had worn the foul garment of transgression, and it covered us from head to foot, even so must He wear the garments of shame and derision from the crown of His head even to the sole of His foot.

"Oh Love, too boundless to be shown
By any but the Lord alone!
O Love offended, which sustains
The bold offender's curse and pains!
O Love, which could no motive have,
But mere benignity to save."

II. Removing the curtain again from this sorrowful spectacle, I see here a SOLEMN WARNING which speaks softly and meltingly to us out of the spectacle of sorrow. Do you ask me what is that warning? It is a warning against our ever committing the same crime as the soldiers did. "The same!" say you; "why, we should never plat a crown of thorns for that dear head." I pray you never may; but there are many who have done, and are doing it. Those are guilty of this crime who, as these soldiers did, *deny His claims*. Busy are the wise men of this world at this very time all over the world, busy in gathering thorns and twisting them, that they may afflict the Lord's Anointed. Some of them cry, "Yes, he was a good man, but not the Son of God"; others even deny His superlative excellence in life and teaching; they cavil at His perfection, and imagine flaws where none exist. Never are they happier than when impugning His character. There are some who ply all their wit, and tax their utmost skill for nothing else but to discover discrepancies in the gospel narratives, or to conjure up differences between their supposed scientific discoveries and the declarations of the Word of God. Full often have they torn their own hands in weaving crowns of thorn for Him, and I fear some of them will have to lie upon a bed of thorns when they come to die, as the result of their displays of scientific research after briers with which to afflict the Lover of mankind.

Oh, that they would cease this useless and malicious trade of weaving crowns of thorns for Him who is the world's only hope, whose religion is the lone star that gilds the midnight of human sorrow, and guides mortal man to the port of peace! Even for the temporal benefits of Christianity the good Jesus should be treated with respect; He has emancipated the slave, and uplifted the down-trodden; His gospel is the charter of liberty, the scourge of tyrants, and the death of priests. Spread it and you spread peace, freedom, order, love, and joy. He is the greatest of philanthropists, the truest friend of man, wherefore then array yourselves against Him, ye who talk of progress and enlightenment? If men did but know Him they would crown Him with diadems of reverent love, more precious than the pearls of Ind, for His reign will usher in the golden age, and even now it softens the rigour of the present, as it has removed the miseries of the past.

This crowning with thorns is wrought in another fashion by *hypocritical professions of allegiance to Him.* These soldiers put a crown on Christ's head, but they did not mean that He should be king; they put a sceptre in His hand, but it was not the substantial ivory rod which signifies real power, it was only a weak and slender reed. Therein they remind us that Christ is mocked by insincere professors. O ye who love Him not in your inmost souls, ye are those who mock Him: but you say, "Wherein have I failed to crown Him? Did I not join the church? Have I not said that I am a believer?" Oh, if your hearts are not right within you, you have only crowned Him with thorns; if you have not given Him your very soul, you have in awful mockery thrust a sceptre of reed into His hand. Your very religion mocks Him. Your lying professions mock Him. Who hath required this at your hands, to tread His courts? You insult Him at His table! You insult Him on your knees! How can you say you love Him, when your hearts are not with Him? If you have never believed in Him, and repented of sin, and yielded obedience to His command, if you do not own Him in your daily life to be both Lord and King, I charge you lay down the profession which is so dishonouring to Him. If He be God, serve Him; if He be King, obey Him; if He be neither, then do not profess to be Christians. Be honest and bring no crown if you do not accept Him as King.

In a measure the same thing may be done by those who are sincere, but through want of watchfulness *walk so as to dishonour their profession.* Here, if I speak rightly, I shall compel every one of you to confess it in your spirits that you stand condemned; for every time that we act according to our sinful flesh we crown the Saviour's head with thorns. Which of us has not done this? Alas, how far have we fallen short of our own ideal! We have hedged Thee about with the briers of our sin. We have been betrayed into angry tempers, so that we have spoken unadvisedly with our lips; or we have been worldly, and loved that which Thou abhorrest, or we have yielded to our passions, and indulged our evil desires.

Do I speak to any backslider whose open sin has dishonoured the cross of Christ? Surely if there be a spark of grace in you, what I am now saying must cut you to the quick, and act like salt upon a raw wound to make your very soul to smart. Do not your ears tingle as I accuse you deliberately of acts of inconsistency which have twisted a thorny crown for our dear Master's head? It is assuredly so, for you have opened the mouths of blasphemers, taught gainsayers to revile Him, grieved the generation of His people, and made many to stumble.

Dear friends, is there not room to look at home in the case of each one of us? As we do so, let us come with the sorrowful and loving penitent, and wash His dear feet with tears of repentance, because we have crowned His head with thorns.

Thus our thorn-crowned Lord and Master stands before us as a sorrowful spectacle, conveying to us a solemn warning.

III. Lifting the veil again, in the person of our tortured and insulted Lord we see TRIUMPHANT ENDURANCE. He could not be conquered. He was victorious even in the hour of deepest shame.

> "He with unflinching heart
> Bore all disgrace and shame,
> And 'mid the keenest smart
> Lov'd on, yea lov'd the same."

He was bearing at that moment, first, *the substitutionary griefs* which were due to Him because He stood in our place, and from bearing them He did not turn aside. We were sinners, and the reward of sin is pain and death, therefore He bore the chastisement of our peace. He was enduring at that time what we ought to have endured, and draining the cup which justice had mingled for us. Did He start back from it? Oh, no. When first He came to drink of that wormwood and gall in the garden He put it to His lips, and the draught seemed for an instant to stagger even His strong spirit. His soul was exceeding sorrowful, even unto death. He was like one demented, tossed to and fro with inward agony. "My Father," said He, "if it be possible, let this cup pass from me." Thrice did He utter that prayer, while every portion of His manhood was the battle-field of legions of griefs. His soul rushed out at every pore to find a vent for its swelling woes, His whole body being covered with gory sweat.

After that tremendous struggle the strength of love mastered the weakness of manhood; He put that cup to His lips and never shrank, but He drank right on till not a dreg was left; and now the cup of wrath is empty, no trace of the terrible wine of the wrath of God can be found within it. At one tremendous draught of love the Lord for ever drank destruction dry for all His people. "Who is he that condemneth? It is Christ that died, yea, rather, that hath risen again," and "there is therefore now no condemnation to them that are in Christ Jesus, who walk not after the flesh but after the Spirit." Now surely endurance had reached a very high point when He was made to endure the painful mockery which our text describes, yet He quailed not, nor removed from His settled purpose. He had undertaken, and

He would go through. Look at Him, and see there a miracle of patient endurance of griefs which would have sent a world to hell had He not borne them on our behalf.

Besides the shame and suffering due for sin, with which it pleased the Father to bruise Him, He was enduring *a superfluity of malice from the hate of men*. Why needed men have concentrated all their scorn and cruelty into His execution? Was it not enough that He must die? Did it give pleasure to their iron hearts to rack His tenderest sensibilities? Wherefore these inventions for deepening His woe? Had any of us been thus derided we should have resented it. There is not a man or woman here who could have been silent under such indignities, but Jesus sat in omnipotence of patience, possessing His soul right royally. Glorious pattern of patience, we adore Thee as we see how malice could not conquer Thine almighty love!

I venture to suggest that such was the picture of patience which our blessed Lord exhibited that it may have moved some even of the soldiery themselves. Has it ever occurred to you to ask how Matthew came to know all about that mockery? Matthew was not there. Mark also gives an account of it, but he would not have been tolerated in the guard-room. The Prætorians were far too proud and rough to tolerate Jews, much less disciples of Jesus, in their common hall. Since there could have been nobody there except the legionaries themselves, it is well to inquire—Who told this tale? It must have been an eyewitness. May it not have been that centurion who in the same chapter is reported to have said, "Certainly this was the Son of God"? May not that scene as well as the Lord's death have led him to that conclusion?

We do not know, but this much is very evident, the story must have been told by an eyewitness, and also by one who sympathised with the sufferer, for to my ear it does not read like the description of an unconcerned spectator. I should not wonder—I would almost venture to assert—that our Lord's marred but patient visage preached such a sermon that one at least who gazed upon it felt its mysterious power, felt that such patience was more than human, and accepted the thorn-crowned Saviour as henceforth his Lord and his King. This I do know, that if you and I want to conquer human hearts for Jesus we must be patient too; and if, when they ridicule and persecute us, we can but endure without repining or retaliation, we shall exercise an influence which even the most brutal will feel, and to which chosen minds will submit themselves.

IV. Drawing up the veil again, I think we have before us, in the fourth place, in the person of the triumphant sufferer, a SACRED MEDICINE. I can only hint at the diseases which it will cure. These blood-besprinkled thorns are plants of renown, precious in heavenly surgery if they be rightly used. Take but a thorn out of this crown and use it as a lancet, and it will let out the hot blood of passion and abate the fever of pride; it is a wonderful remedy for swelling flesh and grievous boils of sin. He who sees Jesus crowned with thorns will loathe to look on self, except it be through tears of contrition. This thorn at the breast will make men sing, but not with notes of self-congratulation, the notes will be those of a dove moaning for her mate. Gideon taught the men of Succoth with thorns, but the lessons were not so salutary as those which we learn from the thorns of Jesus. The sacred medicine which the good Physician brings to us in His thorny chaplet acts as a tonic, and strengthens us to endure without depression whatever shame or loss His service may bring upon us:—

> "Who defeats my fiercest foes?
> Who consoles my saddest woes?
> Who revives my fainting heart,
> Healing all its hidden smart?
> Jesus crowned with thorns."

When you begin to serve God, and for His sake endeavour to benefit your fellow-mortals, do not expect any reward from men, except to be misunderstood, suspected, and abused. The best men in the world are usually the worst spoken of. An evil world cannot speak well of holy lives. The sweetest fruit is most pecked at by the birds, the most heaven-nearing mountain is most beaten by the storms, and the loveliest character is the most assailed. Those whom you would save will not thank you for your anxiety, but blame you for your interference. If you rebuke their sins they will frequently resent your warnings, if you invite them to Jesus, they will make light of your entreaties. Are you prepared for this? If not, consider Him who endured such contradiction of sinners against Himself lest ye be weary and faint in your minds.

The thorn crown is also a remedy for discontent and affliction. When enduring bodily pain we are apt to wince and fret, but if we remember Jesus crowned with thorns, we say—

> "His way was much rougher and darker than mine;
> Did Christ my Lord suffer, and shall I repine?"

And so our complaints grow dumb; for very shame we dare not compare our maladies with His woes. Resignation is learned at Jesus' feet, when we see our great Exemplar made perfect through suffering.

The thorn crown is a cure for care. We would cheerfully wear any array which our Lord may prepare for us, but it is a great folly to plat needless thorn crowns for ourselves. Yet I have seen some who are, I hope, true believers take much trouble to trouble themselves, and labour to increase their own labours. They haste to be rich, they fret, they toil, they worry, and torment themselves to load themselves with the burden of wealth: they wound themselves to wear the thorny crown of worldly greatness. Many are the ways of making rods for our own backs. I have known mothers make thorn crowns out of their children whom they could not trust with God, they have been worn with family anxieties when they might have rejoiced in God. I have known others make thorn crowns out of silly fears, for which there were no grounds whatever; but they seemed ambitious to be fretful, eager to prick themselves with briers. O believer, say to thyself, "My Lord wore my crown of thorns for me; why should I wear it too?" He took our griefs and carried our sorrows that we might be a happy people, and be able to obey the command, "Take no thought for the morrow, for the morrow shall take thought for the things of itself." Ours is the crown of loving kindness and tender mercies, and we wear it when we cast all our care on Him who careth for us.

Who seeks for ease when he has seen the Lord Christ? If Christ wears a crown of thorns, shall we covet a crown of laurel? Even the fierce Crusader when he entered into Jerusalem, and was elected king, had sense enough to say, "I will not wear a crown of gold in the same city where my Saviour wore a crown of thorns." Why should we desire, like feather-bed soldiers, to have everything arranged for our ease and pleasure? Why this reclining upon couches when Jesus hangs on a cross? Why this soft raiment when He is naked? Why these luxuries when He is barbarously entreated? Thus the thorn crown cures us at once of the vainglory of the world, and of our own selfish love of ease. The world's minstrel may cry, "Ho, boy, come hither, and crown me with rose buds!" but the voluptuary's request is not for us. For us neither delights of the flesh nor the pride of life can have charms while the Man of Sorrows is in view. For us it remains to suffer, and to labour, till the King shall bid us share His rest.

V. I must notice in the fifth place that there is before us a MYSTIC CORONATION. Bear with my many divisions. The coronation of Christ with thorns was symbolical, and had great meaning in it, for, first, it was to Him *a triumphal crown.* Christ had fought with sin from the day when He first stood foot to foot with it in the wilderness up to the time when He entered Pilate's hall, and He had conquered it. As a witness that He

had gained the victory behold sin's crown seized as a trophy!
What was the crown of sin? Thorns. These sprang from the
curse. "Thorns also and thistles shall it bring forth to thee,"
was the coronation of sin, and now Christ has taken away its
crown, and put it on His own head. He has spoiled sin of its
richest regalia, and He wears it Himself. Glorious champion,
all hail! What if I say that the thorns constituted a mural
crown? Paradise was set round with a hedge of thorns so sharp
that none could enter it, but our champion leaped first upon the
bristling rampart, and bore the blood-red banner of His cross
into the heart of that better new Eden, which thus He won for
us never to be lost again. Jesus wears the mural chaplet which
denotes that He has opened Paradise.

It was a wrestler's crown He wore, for He wrestled not with
flesh and blood, but with principalities and powers, and He over-
threw His foe. It was a racer's crown He wore, for He had run
with the mighty and outstripped them in the race. He had
well-nigh finished His course, and had but a step or two more to
take to reach the goal. Here is a marvellous field for enlarge-
ment, and we must stay at once lest we go too far. It was
a crown rich with glory, despite the shame which was intended
by it. We see in Jesus the monarch of the realms of misery, the
chief among ten thousand sufferers. Never say, "I am a great
sufferer." What are our griefs compared with His? As the
poet stood upon the Palatine Mount and thought of Rome's
dire ruin, he exclaimed, "What are our woes and sufferings?"
even so I ask, What are our shallow griefs compared with the
infinite sorrows of Immanuel? Well may we "control in our
close breasts our petty misery."

VI. The last word is this. In the thorn crown I see a MIGHTY
STIMULUS. A mighty stimulus to what? Why, first, to fervent
love of Him. Can you see Him crowned with thorns and not
be drawn to Him? Methinks, if He could come among us
this morning, and we could see Him, there would be a loving
press around Him to touch the hem of His garment or to kiss His
feet. Saviour, Thou art very precious to us. Dearest of all the
names above, my Saviour and my God, thou art always glorious,
but in these eyes thou art never more lovely than when arrayed
in shameful mockery. The Lily of the Valley, and the Rose of
Sharon, both in one is He, fair in the perfection of His character,
and blood-red in the greatness of His sufferings. Worship Him!
Adore Him! Bless Him! And let your voices sing "Worthy
the Lamb."

This sight is a stimulus, next, to repentance. Did our sins
put thorns around His head? Oh, my poor fallen nature, I
will scourge thee for scourging Him, and make thee feel the thorns

for causing Him to endure them. What, can you see your best Beloved put to such shame, and yet hold truce or parley with the sins which pierced Him? It cannot be. Let us declare before God our soul's keen grief that we should make the Saviour suffer so; then let us pray for grace to hedge our lives around with thorns that from this very day sin may not approach us.

I thought this day of how ofttimes I have seen the blackthorn growing in the hedge all bristling with a thousand prickles, but right in the centre of the bush have I seen the pretty nest of a little bird. Why did the creature place its habitation there? Because the thorns become a protection to it, and shelter it from harm. As I meditated last night upon this blessed subject, I thought I would bid you build your nests within the thorns of Christ. It is a safe place for sinners. Neither Satan, sin, nor death can reach you there. Gaze on your Saviour's sufferings, and you will see sin atoned for. Fly into His wounds! fly, ye timid trembling doves! there is no resting-place so safe for you. Build your nests, I say again, among these thorns, and when you have done so, and trusted Jesus, and counted Him to be all in all to you, then come and crown His sacred head with other crowns.

What glory does He deserve? What is good enough for Him? If we could take all the precious things from all the treasuries of monarchs, they would not be worthy to be pebbles beneath His feet. If we could bring Him all the sceptres, mitres, tiaras, diadems, and all other pomp of earth, they would be altogether unworthy to be thrown in the dust before Him. Wherewith shall we crown Him? Come let us weave our praises together and set our tears for pearls, our love for gold. They will sparkle like so many diamonds in His esteem, for He loves repentance, and He loves faith. Let us make a chaplet this morning with our praises, and crown Him as the laureate of grace. This day on which He rose from the dead, let us extol Him. Oh, for grace to do it in the heart, and then in the life, and then with the tongue, that we may praise Him for ever who bowed His head to shame for us.

THE AGONY OF GETHSEMANE

A Sermon

Text.—"And being in an agony he prayed more earnestly: and his sweat was as it were great drops of blood falling down to the ground."—Luke xxii. 44.

OUR Lord, after having eaten the passover and celebrated the supper with His disciples, went with them to the Mount of Olives, and entered the garden of Gethsemane. What induced Him to select that place to be the scene of His terrible agony? Why there in preference to anywhere else would He be arrested by His enemies? May we not conceive that as in a garden Adam's self-indulgence ruined us, so in another garden the agonies of the second Adam should restore us? Gethsemane supplies the medicine for the ills which followed upon the forbidden fruit of Eden. No flowers which bloomed upon the banks of the four-fold river were ever so precious to our race as the bitter herbs which grew hard by the black and sullen stream of Kedron.

May not our Lord also have thought of David, when on that memorable occasion he fled out of the city from his rebellious son, and it is written, "The king also himself passed over the brook Kedron," and he and his people went up bare-footed and bare-headed, weeping as they went? Behold, the greater David leaves the temple to become desolate, and forsakes the city which had rejected His admonitions, and with a sorrowful heart crosses the foul brook, to find in solitude a solace for His woes. Our Lord Jesus, moreover, meant us to see that our sin changed every-thing about Him into sorrow, it turned His riches into poverty, His peace into travail, His glory into shame, and so the place of His peaceful retirement, where in hallowed devotion He had been nearest heaven in communion with God, our sin transformed into the focus of His sorrow, the centre of His woe. Where He had enjoyed most, there He must be called to suffer most.

Our Lord may also have chosen the garden, because needing every remembrance that could sustain Him in the conflict, He felt refreshed by the memory of former hours which there had passed away so quietly. He had there prayed, and gained strength and comfort. Those gnarled and twisted olives knew Him well; there was scarce a blade of grass in the garden which

He had not knelt upon; He had consecrated the spot to fellow-ship with God. What wonder then that He preferred this favoured soil? Just as a man would choose in sickness to lie in his own bed, so Jesus chose to endure His agony in His own oratory, where the recollections of former communings with His Father would come vividly before Him.

But, probably, the chief reason for His resort to Gethsemane was, that it was His well-known haunt, and John tells us, "Judas also knew the place." Our Lord did not wish to conceal Himself, He did not need to be hunted down like a thief, or searched out by spies. He went boldly to the place where His enemies knew that He was accustomed to pray, for He was willing to be taken to suffering and to death. They did not drag Him off to Pilate's hall against His will, but He went with them volun-tarily. When the hour was come for Him to be betrayed there was He in a place where the traitor could readily find Him, and when Judas would betray Him with a kiss His cheek was ready to receive the traitorous salutation. The blessed Saviour delighted to do the will of the Lord, though it involved obedience unto death.

We have thus come to the gate of the garden of Gethsemane, let us now enter; but first let us put off our shoe from our foot, as Moses did, when he also saw the bush which burned with fire, and was not consumed. Surely we may say with Jacob, "How dreadful is this place!"

Meditating upon the agonizing scene in Gethsemane we are compelled to observe that our Saviour there endured a grief unknown to any previous period of His life, and therefore we will commence our discourse by raising the question, WHAT WAS THE CAUSE OF THE PECULIAR GRIEF OF GETHSEMANE? Our Lord was the "Man of sorrows and acquainted with grief" throughout His whole life, and yet, though it may sound paradoxical, I scarcely think there existed on the face of the earth a happier man than Jesus of Nazareth, for the griefs which He endured were counterbalanced by the peace of purity, the calm of fellow-ship with God, and the joy of benevolence. This last every good man knows to be very sweet, and all the sweeter in propor-tion to the pain which is voluntarily endured for the carrying out of its kind designs. It is always joy to do good, cost what it may.

Moreover Jesus dwelt at perfect peace with God at all times; we know that He did so, for He regarded that peace as a choice legacy which He could bequeath to His disciples, and ere He died He said to them, "Peace I leave with you, my peace I give unto you." He was meek and lowly of heart, and therefore His soul had rest; He was one of the meek who inherit the earth;

one of the peacemakers who are and must be blessed. I think I mistake not when I say that our Lord was far from being an unhappy man. But in Gethsemane all seems changed, His peace is gone, His calm is turned to tempest. After supper our Lord had sung a hymn, but there was no singing in Gethsemane. Adown the steep bank which led from Jerusalem to the Kedron He talked very cheerfully, saying, "I am the vine and ye are the branches," and that wondrous prayer which He prayed with His disciples after that discourse, is very full of majesty: "Father, I will that they also whom thou hast given me be with me where I am," is a very different prayer from that inside Gethsemane's walls, where He cries, "If it be possible, let this cup pass from me."

Notice that all His life long you scarcely find Him uttering an expression of grief, and yet here He says, not only by His sighs and by His bloody sweat, but in so many words, "My soul is exceeding sorrowful even unto death." In the garden the sufferer could not conceal His grief, and does not appear to have wished to do so. Backward and forward thrice He ran to His disciples, He let them see His sorrow and appealed to them for sympathy; His exclamations were very piteous, and His sighs and groans were, I doubt not, very terrible to hear. Chiefly did that sorrow reveal itself in bloody sweat, which is a very unusual phenomenon, although I suppose we must believe those writers who record instances somewhat similar. The old physician Galen gives an instance in which, through extremity of horror, an individual poured forth a discoloured sweat, so nearly crimson as at any rate to appear to have been blood. Other cases are given by medical authorities. We do not, however, on any previous occasion observe anything like this in our Lord's life; it was only in the last grim struggle among the olive trees that our champion resisted unto blood, agonizing against sin. What ailed Thee, O Lord, that Thou shouldst be so sorely troubled just then?

We are clear that His deep sorrow and distress were not occasioned by any bodily pain. Our Saviour had doubtless been familiar with weakness and pain, for He took our sicknesses, but He never in any previous instance complained of physical suffering. Neither at the time when He entered Gethsemane had He been grieved by any bereavement. We know why it is written "Jesus wept," it was because His friend Lazarus was dead; but here there was no funeral, nor sick bed, nor particular cause of grief in that direction. Nor was it the revived remembrance of any past reproaches which had lain dormant in His mind. Long before this "reproach had broken His heart," and He had known to the full the vexations of contumely and scorn. They had called Him a "drunken man and a wine bibber," they had charged Him with casting out devils by the prince of the devils; they could not say more and yet He had bravely faced it all, it could not be possible that He was now sorrowful unto death for such a cause. There must have been a something sharper than pain, more cutting than reproach, more terrible than bereavement, which now at this time grappled with the Saviour, and made Him "exceeding sorrowful, and very heavy."

Do you suppose it was the fear of coming scorn, or the dread of crucifixion? Was it terror at the thought of death? Is not such a supposition impossible? Every man dreads death, and as man Jesus could not but shrink from it. When we were originally made we were created for immortality, and therefore to die is strange and uncongenial work to us, and the instincts of self-preservation cause us to start back from it; but surely in our Lord's case that natural cause could not have produced such specially painful results. It does not make even such poor cowards as we are sweat great drops of blood, why then should it work such terror in him? It is dishonouring to our Lord to imagine Him less brave than His own disciples, yet we have seen some of the very feeblest of His saints triumphant in the prospect of departing.

Read the stories of the martyrs, and you will frequently find them exultant in the near approach of the most cruel sufferings. The joy of the Lord has given such strength to them, that no coward thought has alarmed them for a single moment, but they have gone to the stake, or to the block, with psalms of victory upon their lips. Our Master must not be thought of as inferior to His boldest servants, it cannot be that He should tremble where they were brave. Oh, no; the noblest spirit among yon martyr-band is the Leader Himself, who in suffering and heroism surpassed them all; none could so defy the pangs of death as the Lord Jesus, who, for the joy which was set before Him, endured the cross, despising the shame.

What is it then, think you, that so peculiarly marks off Gethsemane and the griefs thereof? We believe that now the Father put Him to grief for us. It was now that our Lord had to take a certain cup *from the Father's hand.* Not from the Jews, not from the traitor Judas, not from the sleeping disciples, not from the devil came the trial now, but it was a cup filled by one whom He knew to be His Father, but who nevertheless He understood to have appointed Him a very bitter potion, a cup not to be drunk by His body and to spend its gall upon His flesh, but a cup which specially amazed His soul and troubled His inmost heart. He shrunk from it, and therefore be ye sure that it was a draught more dreadful than physical pain, since from that He did not shrink; it was a potion more dreadful than reproach, from that He had not turned aside; more dreadful than Satanic temptation,—*that* He had overcome: it was a something inconceivably terrible, amazingly full of dread, which came from the Father's hand. This removes all doubt as to what it was, for we read "It pleased the Lord to bruise him, he hath put him to grief: when thou shalt make his soul an offering for sin." "The Lord hath made to meet on him the iniquity of us all." He hath made Him to be sin for us though He knew no sin. This, then, is that which caused the Saviour such extraordinary depression. He was now about to "taste death for every man," to bear the curse which was due to sinners, because He stood in the sinner's place and must suffer in the sinner's stead. Here is the secret of those agonies which it is not possible for me to set forth in order before you, so true is it that—

> "'Tis to God, and God alone,
>   That His griefs are fully known."

Yet would I exhort you to consider these griefs awhile, that you may love the sufferer. He now realized, perhaps for the first time, what it was to be a sin bearer. As God He was perfectly holy and incapable of sin, and as man He was without original taint and spotlessly pure; yet He had to bear sin, to be led forth as the scapegoat bearing the iniquity of Israel upon His head, to be taken and made a sin offering, and as a loathsome thing (for nothing was more loathsome than the sin offering) to be taken without the camp and utterly consumed with the fire of divine wrath. Do you wonder that His infinite purity started back from that? Would He have been what He was if it had not been a very solemn thing for Him to stand before God in the position of a sinner? yea, and as Luther would have said it, to be looked upon by God as if He were all the sinners in the world, and as if He had committed all the sin that ever had been committed by His people, for it was all laid on Him, and on Him must the vengeance due for it all be poured; He must be the centre of all the vengeance and bear away upon Himself what ought to have fallen upon the guilty sons of men. To stand in such a position when once it was realised must have been very terrible to the Redeemer's holy soul.

Then, too, no doubt the penalty of sin began to be realised by Him in the Garden—first the sin which had put Him in the position of a suffering substitute, and then the penalty which must be borne, because He was in that position. I dread to the last degree that kind of theology which is so common now-a-days, which seeks to depreciate and diminish our estimate of the

sufferings of our Lord Jesus Christ. Brethren, that was no
trifling suffering which made recompense to the justice of God
for the sins of men. I am never afraid of exaggeration, when I
speak of what my Lord endured. All hell was distilled into that
cup, of which our God and Saviour Jesus Christ was made to
drink. It was not eternal suffering, but since He was divine
He could in a short time offer unto God a vindication of His
justice which sinners in hell could not have offered had they been
left to suffer in their own persons for ever. To be treated as a
sinner, to be smitten as a sinner, though in Him was no sin,—this
it was which caused Him the agony of which our text speaks.

Having thus spoken of the cause of His peculiar grief, I think
we shall be able to support our view of the matter, while we lead
you to consider, WHAT WAS THE CHARACTER OF THE GRIEF ITSELF?
I shall trouble you, as little as possible, with the Greek words
used by the evangelists; I have studied each one of them, to try
and find out the shades of their meaning, but it will suffice if
I give you the results of my careful investigations. What was the
grief itself? How was it described? This great sorrow assailed
our Lord some four days before He suffered. If you turn to
John xii. 27, you find that remarkable utterance, "Now is my
soul troubled." We never knew Him say that before. This
was a foretaste of the great depression of spirit which was so
soon to lay Him prostrate in Gethsemane. "Now is my soul
troubled; and what shall I say? Father, save me from this
hour; but for this cause came I unto this hour."

After that we read of Him in Matthew xxvi. 37, that "he began
to be sorrowful and very heavy." The depression had come over
Him again. It was not pain, it was not a palpitation of the heart,
or an aching of the brow, it was worse than these. Trouble of
spirit is worse than pain of body; pain may bring trouble and
be the incidental cause of sorrow, but if the mind is perfectly
untroubled, how well a man can bear pain, and when the soul is
exhilarated and lifted up with inward joy pain of body is almost
forgotten, the soul conquering the body. On the other hand
the soul's sorrow will create bodily pain, the lower nature sympa-
thizing with the higher. Our Lord's main suffering lay in His
soul—His soul-sufferings were the soul of His sufferings. "A
wounded spirit who can bear?" Pain of spirit is the worst of
pain, sorrow of heart is the climax of griefs. Let those who have
ever known sinking spirits, despondency, and mental gloom,
attest the truth of what I say!

This sorrow of heart appears to have led to a very deep depression of our Lord's spirit. In the 26th of Matthew, 37th verse,
you find it recorded that he was "*very heavy,*" and that expression
is full of meaning,—of more meaning, indeed, than it would be

H

easy to explain. The word in the original is a very difficult one to translate. It may signify the abstraction of the mind, and its complete occupation by sorrow, to the exclusion of every thought which might have alleviated the distress. One burning thought consumed His whole soul, and burned up all that might have yielded comfort. For awhile His mind refused to dwell upon the result of His death, the consequent joy which was set before Him. His position as a sinbearer, and the desertion by His Father which was necessitated thereby, engrossed His contemplations and hurried His soul away from all else. Some have seen in the word a measure of distraction, and though I will not go far in that direction, yet it does seem as if our Saviour's mind underwent perturbations and convulsions widely different from His usual calm, collected spirit. He was tossed to and fro as upon a mighty sea of trouble, which was wrought to tempest, and carried Him away in its fury. "We did esteem him stricken, smitten of God and afflicted." As the psalmist said, innumerable evils compassed Him about so that His heart failed Him. He was "very heavy." The learned Thomas Goodwin says, "The word denotes a failing, deficiency, and sinking of spirit, such as happens to men in sickness and swounding." Epaphroditus' sickness, whereby he was brought near to death, is called by the same word; so that, we see, that Christ's soul was sick and fainted. Was not His sweat produced by exhaustion? The cold, clammy sweat of dying men comes through faintness of body, but the bloody sweat of Jesus came from an utter faintness and prostration of soul. He was in an awful soul-swoon, and suffered an inward death, whose accompaniment was not watery tears from the eyes, but a weeping of blood from the entire man.

Mark tells us next, in his fourteenth chapter and thirty-third verse, that our Lord was "*sore amazed.*" The Greek word does not merely import that he was astonished and surprised, but that His amazement went to an extremity of horror, such as men fall into when their hair stands on end and their flesh trembles. As the delivery of the law made Moses exceedingly fear and quake, and as David said, "My flesh trembleth because of thy judgments," so our Lord was stricken with horror at the sight of the sin which was laid upon Him and the vengeance which was due on account of it. The Saviour was first "sorrowful," then depressed, and "heavy," and lastly, sore amazed and filled with amazement; for even He as a man could scarce have known what it was that He had undertaken to bear. He had looked at it calmly and quietly, and felt that whatever it was He would bear it for our sake; but when it actually came to the bearing of sin He was utterly astonished and taken aback at the dreadful position of standing in the sinner's place before God, of having His holy Father look upon Him as the sinner's representative, and of being forsaken by that Father with whom He had lived on terms of amity and delight from old eternity. It staggered His holy, tender, loving nature, and He was "sore amazed" and was "very heavy."

We are further taught that there surrounded, encompassed, and overwhelmed Him an ocean of sorrow, for the thirty-eighth verse of the twenty-sixth of Matthew contains the word *peri-lupos*, which signifies an encompassing around with sorrows. Above Him, beneath Him, around Him, without Him, and within, all, all was anguish, neither was there one alleviation or source of consolation. His disciples could not help Him,—they were all but one sleeping, and he who was awake was on the road to betray Him. His spirit cried out in the presence of the Almighty God beneath the crushing burden and unbearable load of His miseries. No griefs could have gone further than Christ's, and He Himself said, "My soul is *exceeding sorrowful*," or surrounded with sorrow "even unto death." He did not die in the garden, but He suffered as much as if He had died.

Luke, to crown all, tells us in our text, that our Lord was *in an agony.* The expression "agony" signifies a conflict, a contest, a wrestling. With whom was the agony? With whom did He wrestle? I believe it was with Himself; the contest here intended was not with His God; no, "not as I will but as thou wilt" does not look like wrestling with God; it was not a contest with Satan, for, as we have already seen, He would not have been so sore amazed had that been the conflict, but it was a terrible combat within Himself, an agony within His own soul. Remember that He could have escaped from all this grief with one resolve of His will, and naturally the manhood in Him said, "Do not bear it!" and the purity of His heart said, "Oh do not bear it, do not stand in the place of the sinner"; and the delicate sensitiveness of His mysterious nature shrank altogether from any form of connection with sin; yet infinite love said, "Bear it, stoop beneath the load"; and so there was agony between the attributes of His nature, a battle on an awful scale in the arena of His soul. The purity which cannot bear to come into contact with sin must have been very mighty in Christ, while the love which would not let His people perish was very mighty too.

It was a struggle on a Titanic scale, as if a Hercules had met another Hercules; two tremendous forces strove and fought and agonised within the bleeding heart of Jesus. Nothing causes a man more torture than to be dragged hither and thither with contending emotions; as civil war is the worst and most cruel kind of war, so a war within a man's soul when two great passions in him struggle for the mastery, and both noble passions too, causes a trouble and distress which none but he that feels it can understand. I marvel not that our Lord's sweat was as it were great drops of blood, when such an inward pressure made Him like a cluster trodden in the wine-press.

Our third question shall be, WHAT WAS OUR LORD'S SOLACE IN ALL THIS? He sought help in human companionship, and very natural it was that He should do so. God has created in our human nature a craving for sympathy. We do not amiss when we expect our brethren to watch with us in our hour of trial; but our Lord did not find that men were able to assist Him; however willing their spirit might be, their flesh was weak. What, then, did He do? He resorted to prayer, and especially to prayer to God under the character of Father. I have learned by experience that we never know the sweetness of the Fatherhood of God so much as when we are in very bitter anguish; I can understand why the Saviour said "Abba, Father," it was anguish that brought Him down as a chastened child to appeal plaintively to a Father's love. In the bitterness of my soul I have cried, "If, indeed, Thou be my Father, by the bowels of Thy fatherhood have pity on Thy child"; and here Jesus pleads with His Father as we have done, and finds comfort in that pleading. Prayer was the channel of the Redeemer's comfort, earnest, intense, reverent, repeated prayer, and after each time of prayer He seems to have grown quiet, and to have gone to His disciples with a measure of restored peace of mind. The sight of their sleeping helped to bring back His griefs, and therefore He returned to pray again, and each time He was comforted, so that when He had prayed for the third time He was prepared to meet Judas and the soldiers and to go with silent patience to judgment and to death. His great comfort was prayer and submission to the divine will, for when He had laid His own will down at His Father's feet the feebleness of His flesh spoke no more complainingly, but in sweet silence, like a sheep dumb before her shearers, He contained His soul in patience and rest. Dear brothers and sisters, if any of you shall have your Gethsemane and your heavy griefs, imitate your Master by resorting to prayer, by crying to your Father, and by learning submission to His will.

I shall conclude by drawing two or three inferences from the whole subject. May the Holy Spirit instruct us.

The first is this—Learn, dear brethren, *the real humanity of our Lord Jesus Christ*. Do not think of Him as God merely, though He is assuredly divine, but feel Him to be near of kin to you, bone of your bone, flesh of your flesh. How thoroughly can He sympathize with you! He has been burdened with all your burdens and grieved with all your griefs. Are the waters very deep through which you are passing? Yet they are not deep compared with the torrents with which He was buffeted. Never a pang penetrates your spirit to which your covenant Head was a stranger. Jesus can sympathize with you in all your sorrows, for He has suffered far more than you have ever suffered, and is able therefore to succour you in your temptations. Lay hold on Jesus as your familiar friend, your brother born for adversity, and you will have obtained a consolation which will bear you through the uttermost deeps.

Next *see here the intolerable evil of sin.* You are a sinner, which Jesus never was, yet even to stand in the sinner's place was so dreadful to Him that He was sorrowful even unto death. What will sin one day be to you if you should be found guilty at the last! Oh, could we tell the horror of sin there is not one among us that would be satisfied to remain in sin for a single moment; I believe there would go up from this house of prayer this morning a weeping and a wailing such as might be heard in the very streets, if men and women here who are living in sin could really know what sin is, and what the wrath of God is that rests upon them, and what the judgments of God will be that will shortly surround them and destroy them. Oh soul, sin must be an awful thing if it so crushed our Lord. If the very imputation of it fetched bloody sweat from the pure and holy Saviour, what must sin itself be? Avoid it, pass not by it, turn away from the very appearance of it, walk humbly and carefully with your God that sin may not harm you, for it is an exceeding plague, an infinite pest.

Learn next, but oh how few minutes have I in which to speak of such a lesson, *the matchless love of Jesus,* that for your sakes and mine He would not merely suffer in body, but consented even to bear the horror of being accounted a sinner, and coming under the wrath of God because of our sins although it cost Him suffering unto death and sore amazement, yet sooner than that we shall perish, the Lord smarted as our surety. Can we not cheerfully endure persecution for His sake? Can we not labour earnestly for Him? Are we so ungenerous that His cause shall know a lack while we have the means of helping it? Are we so base that His work shall flag while we have strength to carry it on? I charge you by Gethsemane, my brethren, if you have a part and lot in the passion of your Saviour, love Him much who loved you so immeasurably, and spend and be spent for Him.

Again looking at Jesus in the garden, we learn the *excellence and completeness of the atonement.* How black I am, how filthy, how loathsome in the sight of God,—I feel myself only fit to be cast into the lowest hell, and I wonder that God has not long ago cast me there; but I go into Gethsemane, and I peer under those gnarled olive trees, and I see my Saviour. Yes, I see Him wallowing on the ground in anguish, and hear such groans come from Him as never came from human breast before. I look upon the earth and see it red with His blood, while His face is smeared with gory sweat, and I say to myself, "My God, my Saviour, what aileth thee?" I hear Him reply, "I am suffering for thy sin," and then I take comfort, for while I fain would have spared my Lord such an anguish, now that the anguish is over I can understand how Jehovah can spare me, because He smote His Son in my stead.

Now I have hope of justification, for I bring before the justice of God and my own conscience the remembrance of my bleeding Saviour, and I say, Canst Thou twice demand payment, first at the hand of Thy agonising Son and then again at mine? Sinner as I am, I stand before the burning throne of the severity of God, and am not afraid of it. Canst thou scorch me, O consuming fire, when thou hast not only scorched but utterly consumed my substitute? Nay, by faith, my soul sees justice satisfied, the law honoured, the moral government of God established, and yet my once guilty soul absolved and set free. The fire of avenging justice has spent itself, and the law has exhausted its most rigorous demands upon the person of Him who was made a curse for us, that we might be made the righteousness of God in Him. Oh the sweetness of the comfort which flows from the atoning blood! Obtain that comfort, my brethren, and never leave it. Cling to your Lord's bleeding heart, and drink in abundant consolation.

Last of all, *what must be the terror of the punishment which will fall upon those men who reject the atoning blood,* and who will have to stand before God in their own proper persons to suffer for their sins. I will tell you, sir, with pain in my heart as I tell you it, what will happen to those of you who reject my Lord. Jesus Christ my Lord and Master is a sign and prophecy to you of what will happen to you. Not in a garden, but on that bed of yours where you have so often been refreshed, you will be surprised and overtaken, and the pains of death will get hold upon you. With an exceeding sorrow and remorse for your misspent life and for a rejected Saviour you will be made very heavy. Then will your darling sin, your favourite lust, like another Judas, betray you with a kiss. While yet your soul lingers on your lip you will be seized and taken off by a body of evil ones, and carried away to the bar of God, just as Jesus was taken to the judgment seat of Caiaphas. There shall be a speedy, personal, and somewhat private judgment, by which you shall be committed to prison where, in darkness and weeping, and wailing, you shall

spend the night before the great assize of the judgment morning.
Then shall the day break and the resurrection morning come, and
as our Lord then appeared before Pilate, so will you appear
before the highest tribunal, not that of Pilate, but the dread
judgment seat of the Son of God, whom you have despised and
rejected. Then will witnesses come against you, not false witnesses, but true, and you will stand speechless, even as Jesus
said not a word before His accusers. Then will conscience and
despair buffet you, until you will become such a monument of
misery, such a spectacle of contempt, as to be fitly noted by
another *Ecce Homo*, and men shall look at you, and say "Behold
the man and the suffering which has come upon him, because
he despised his God and found pleasure in sin." Then shall
you be condemned. "Depart, ye cursed," shall be your sentence, even as "Let him be crucified" was the doom of Jesus.
You shall be taken away by the officers of justice to your doom.
To your shame, and to the confusion of your nakedness, shall
you that have despised the Saviour be made a spectacle of the
justice of God for ever. It is right it should be so, justice rightly
demands it. Sin made the Saviour suffer an agony, shall it
not make you suffer? Moreover, in addition to your sin, you
have rejected the Saviour; you have said, "He shall not be my
trust and confidence." Voluntarily, presumptuously, and against
your own conscience you have refused eternal life; and if you die
rejecting mercy what can come of it but that first your sin, and
secondly your unbelief, shall condemn you to misery without
limit or end. Let Gethsemane warn you, let its groans, and
tears, and bloody sweat admonish you. Repent of sin, and
believe in Jesus. May His Spirit enable you, for Jesus' sake.
Amen.

THREE CROSSES

A Sermon

Text.—"But God forbid that I should glory, save in the cross of our Lord Jesus Christ, by whom the world is crucified unto me, and I unto the world."—Galatians vi. 14.

WHENEVER we rebuke other people we should be prepared to clear ourselves of their offence. The apostle had been rebuking those who wished to glory in the flesh. In denouncing false teachers and upbraiding their weak-minded followers he used sharp language, while he appealed to plain facts and maintained his ground with strong arguments; and this he did without fear of being met by a flank movement, and being charged with doing the same things himself. Very fitly, therefore, does he contrast his own determined purpose with their plausible falseness. They were for making a fair show in the flesh, but he shrunk not from the deepest shame of the Christian profession; nay, so far from shrinking, he even counted it honour to be scorned for Christ's sake, exclaiming, "God forbid that I should glory, save in the cross of our Lord Jesus Christ."

The Galatians, and all others to whom his name was familiar, well knew how truly he spoke; for the manner of his life as well as the matter of his teaching had supplied evidence of this assertion, which none of his foemen could gainsay. There had not been in all his ministry any doctrine that he extolled more highly than this of "Christ crucified"; nor any experience that he touched on more tenderly than this "fellowship with Christ in his sufferings"; nor any rule of conduct that he counted more safe than this following in the footsteps of Him who "endured the cross, despising the shame, and is set down at the right hand of the throne of God." His example accorded with His precept. God grant, of His grace, that there may always be with us the like transparent consistency.

The apostle in the present case warms with emotion at the thought of anybody presuming to set a carnal ordinance in front of the cross, by wishing to glory in circumcision or any other outward institution. The idea of a ceremony claiming to be made more of than faith in Jesus provoked him, till his heart presently grew hot with indignation, and he thundered forth the words, "God forbid!" He never used the sacred name with lightness; but when the fire was hot within him he called God to witness that he did not, and could not, glory in anything but the cross.

Indeed, there is to every true-hearted believer something shocking and revolting in the putting of anything before Jesus Christ, be it what it may, whether it be an idol of superstition or a toy of scepticism, whether it be the fruit of tradition or the flower of philosophy. Do you want new Scriptures to supplement the true sayings of God? Do you want a new Saviour who can surpass Him whom the Father hath sealed? Do you want a new sacrifice that can save you from sins which His atoning blood could not expiate? Do you want a modern song to supersede the new song of "Worthy is the Lamb that was slain"? "O foolish Galatians!" said Paul.

The cross was the centre of his hopes; around it his affections twined; there he had found peace to his troubled conscience. God forbid that he should allow it to be trampled on. Besides, it was the theme of his ministry. "Christ crucified" had already proved the power of God to salvation to every soul who had believed the life-giving message as he proclaimed it in every city. Would any of you, he asks, cast a slur on the cross—you who have been converted—you before whose eyes Jesus Christ hath been evidently set forth crucified among you? How his eyes flash; how his lips quiver; how his heart grows hot within him; with what vehemence he protests: "God forbid that I should glory, save in the cross of our Lord Jesus Christ." He spreads his eagle wing, and rises into eloquence at once, while still his keen eye looks fiercely upon every enemy of the cross whom he leaves far beneath. Oftentimes in his epistles you observe this. He burns, he glows, he mounts, he soars, he is carried clean away as soon as his thoughts are in fellowship with his Lord Jesus, that meek and patient Sufferer, who offered Himself a sacrifice for our sins. When his tongue begins to speak of the glorious work which the Christ of God has done for the sons of men it finds a sudden liberty, and he becomes as "a hind let loose; he giveth goodly words."

Let us, then, in that spirit approach our text; and we notice at once three crucifixions. These are the summary of the text. "God forbid that I should glory, save in the cross of our Lord Jesus Christ"; that is, *Christ crucified.* "By whom," or, "by which" (read it whichever way you like), "the world is crucified unto me"; that is, *a crucified world.* "And I unto the world"; that is, *Paul himself, or the believer, crucified with Christ.* I see again, Calvary before me with its three crosses—Christ in the centre, and on either side of Him a crucified person: one who dies to feel the second death, and another who dies to be with Him in paradise. At these three crosses let us proceed to look.

I. First, then, the main part of our subject lies in CHRIST CRUCIFIED, in whom Paul gloried. I call your attention to the language; "God forbid that I should glory, save in the cross." Some popular authors and public speakers, when they have to state a truth, count it necessary to clothe it in very delicate language. They, perhaps, do not quite intend to conceal its point and edge; but, at any rate, they do not want the projecting angles and bare surfaces of the truth to be too observable, and therefore they cast a cloak around it; they are careful to scabbard the sword of the Spirit. The apostle Paul might have done so here, if he had chosen, but he disdains the artifice. He presents the truth "in the worst possible form," as his opponents say—"in all its naked hideousness," as the Jew would have it; for he does not say, "God forbid that I should glory, save in the *death* of Christ"; but in the *cross*. *You* do not realize, I think—we cannot do so in these days—how the use of that word "cross" would grate on ears refined in Galatia and elsewhere. In those days it meant the felon's tree, the hangman's gibbet; and the apostle, therefore, does not hesitate to put it just so: "Save in that gibbet on which my Master died." We have become so accustomed to associate the name of "the cross" with other sentiments that it does not convey to us that sense of disgrace which it would inflict upon those who heard Paul speak. A family sensitively shrinks if one of its members has been hanged; and much the same would be the natural feeling of one who was told that his leader was crucified. Paul puts it thus badly, he lets it jar thus harshly, though it may prove to some a stumbling-block, and to others foolishness; but he will not cloak it, he glories in "*the cross!*"

On the other hand, I earnestly entreat you to observe how he seems to contrast the glory of the person with the shame of the suffering; for it is not simply the death of Christ, nor of Jesus, nor of Jesus Christ, nor of *the* Lord Jesus Christ, but of "*our Lord Jesus Christ*." Every word tends to set forth the excellence of His person, the majesty of His character, and the interest which all the saints have in Him. It *was* a cross, but it was the cross of our Lord: let us worship Him! It was the cross of our Lord Jesus the Saviour: let us love Him! It was the cross of our Jesus Christ the anointed Messiah: let us reverence Him! Let us sit at His feet and learn of Him! Each one may say, "It was the cross of *my* Lord Jesus Christ"; but it sweetens the whole matter, and gives a largeness to it when we say, "It was the cross of *our* Lord Jesus Christ." Oh yes, we delight to think of the contrast between the precious Christ and the painful cross, the Son of

God and the shameful gibbet. He was Immanuel, God with us; yet did He die the felon's death upon the accursed tree. Paul brings out the shame with great sharpness, and the glory with great plainness. He does not hesitate in either case, whether he would declare the sufferings of Christ or the glory which should follow.

What did he mean, however, by the cross? Of course he cared nothing for the particular piece of wood to which those blessed hands and feet were nailed, for that was mere materialism, and has perished out of mind. He means the glorious doctrine of justification—free justification—through the atoning sacrifice of Jesus Christ. This is what he means by the cross—the expiation for sin which our Lord Jesus Christ made by His death, and the gift of eternal life freely bestowed on all those who by grace are led to trust in Him. To Paul the cross meant just what the brazen serpent meant to Moses. As the brazen serpent in the wilderness was the hope of the sin-bitten, and all that Moses had to do was to bid them look and live, so to-day the cross of Christ—the atonement of Jesus Christ—is the hope of mankind, and our mission is continually to cry, "Look and live! Look and live!"

It is this doctrine, this gospel of Christ crucified, at which the present age, with all its vaunted culture and all its vain philosophies, sneers so broadly, it is this doctrine wherein we glory. We are not ashamed to put it very definitely: we glory in substitution, in the vicarious sacrifice of Jesus in our stead. He was "made sin for us who knew no sin, that we might be made the righteousness of God in him." "All we like sheep have gone astray; we have turned every one to his own way; and the Lord hath laid on Him the iniquity of us all." "Christ hath redeemed us from the curse of the law, being made a curse for us: for it is written, Cursed is every one that hangeth on a tree." We believe in the imputation of sin to the innocent person of our covenant Head and Representative, in the bearing of the penalty by that substituted One, and the clearing by faith of those for whom He bore the punishment of sin.

Now we glory in this. We glory in it, not as men sometimes boast in a creed which they have received by tradition from their forefathers, for we have learned this truth, each one for himself by the inward teaching of the Holy Ghost, and therefore it is very dear to us. We glory in it with no empty boast, but to the inward satisfaction of our own hearts; we prove that satisfaction by the devout consecration of our lives to make it known. We have trusted our souls to its truth. If it be a fable our hopes are for ever shipwrecked, our all is embarked in that venture. We are quite prepared to run that risk, content to perish if this salvation should fail us. We live upon this faith. It is our meat and our drink. Take this away there is nothing left us in the Bible worth the having. It has become to us the head and front of our confidence, our hope, our rest, our joy. Instead of being ashamed to preach it, we wish that we could stand somewhere where all the inhabitants of the earth should hear us, and we would thunder it out day and night. So far from being ashamed of acknowledging it, we count it to be our highest honour and our greatest delight to tell it abroad, as we have opportunity, among the sons of men.

But why do we rejoice in it? Why do we glory in it? The answer is so large that I cannot do more than glance at its manifold claims on our gratitude. In the cross of Christ we glory, because we regard it as a matchless exhibition of the attributes of God. We see there the love of God desiring a way by which He might save mankind, aided by His wisdom, so that a plan is perfected by which the deed can be done without violation of truth and justice. In the cross we see a strange conjunction of what once appeared to be two opposite qualities—justice and mercy. We see how God is supremely just; as just as if He had no mercy, and yet infinitely merciful in the gift of His Son. Mercy and justice in fact become counsel upon the same side, and irresistibly plead for the acquittal of the believing sinner. We can never tell which of the attributes of God shines most glorious in the sacrifice of Christ; they each one find a glorious high throne in the person and work of the Lamb of God that taketh away the sin of the world. Since it has become, as it were, the disk which reflects the character and perfections of God it is meet that we should glory in the cross of Christ; and none shall stay us of our boasting.

We glory in it, next, as the manifestation of the love of Jesus. He was loving inasmuch as He came to earth at all; loving in feeding the hungry, in healing the sick, in raising the dead. He was loving in His whole life: He was embodied charity, the Prince of philanthropists, the King of kindly souls. But oh, His death! —His cruel and shameful death—bearing, as we believe He did, the wrath due to sin, subjecting Himself to the curse, though in Him was no sin—this shows the love of Christ at its highest altitude, and therefore do we glory in it, and will never be ashamed to do so.

We glory in the cross, moreover, because it is the putting away of sin. There was no other way of making an end of sin, and making reconciliation for iniquity. To forgive the transgressions without exacting the penalty would have been contrary to all the threatenings of God. It would not have appeased the claims of justice, nor satisfied the conscience of the sinner.

No peace of mind can be enjoyed without pardon, and con-science declares that no pardon can be obtained without an atonement. We should have distracted ourselves with the fear that it was only a reprieve, and not a remission, even if the most comforting promises had been given unsealed with the atoning blood. The instincts of nature have convinced men of this truth, for all the world over religion has been associated with sacrifice. Almost every kind of worship that has ever sprung up among the sons of men has had sacrifice for its most prominent feature; crime must be avenged, evil and sin cry from the ground, and a victim is sought to avert the vengeance. The heart craves for something that can calm the conscience: that craving is a relic of the ancient truth learned by man in primeval ages.

Now, Christ did make His soul an offering for sin, when His own self He bare our sins in His own body on the tree. With His expiring breath He said, "It is finished!" Oh, wondrous grace! Pardon is now freely published among the sons of men, pardon of which we see the justice and validity. As far as the east is from the west, so far hath God removed our transgressions from us by the death of Christ. This and this alone will put away sin, therefore in this cross of Christ we glory; yea, and in it alone will we glory evermore.

It has put away our sins, blessed be God, so that this load and burden no more weigh us down! We do not speak at random now. It has breathed hope and peace and joy into our spirits. I am sure that no one knows how to glory in the cross unless he has had an experimental acquaintance with its peace-breathing power. I speak what I do know, and testify what I have felt. The burden of my sin laid so heavy upon me that I would sooner have died than have lived. Many a day, and many a night, I felt the flames of hell in the anguish of my heart, because I knew my guilt, but saw no way of righteous forgiveness.

Yet in a moment the load went from me, and I felt overflowing love to the Saviour. I fell at His feet awe-stricken that ever he should have taken away my sin and made an end of it. That matchless deed of love won my heart to Jesus. He changed my nature and renewed my soul in that same hour. But, oh, the joy I had! Those who have sunk to the very depths of des-pair, and risen in a moment to the heights of peace and joy unspeakable, can tell you that they must glory in the cross and its power to save. Why, sirs, we must believe according to our own conscience. We cannot belie that inward witness. We only wish that others had been as deeply convinced of sin, and as truly led to the cross to feel their burden roll from off their shoulder as we have been, and then they, too, would glory in the cross of Christ. Since then we have gone with this remedy in our hands to souls that have been near despair, and we have never found the medicine to fail.

Yet we should not glory so much in the cross, were we not convinced that it is the greatest moral power in all the world. We glory in the cross because it gets at men's hearts when nothing else can reach them. The story of the dying Saviour's love has often impressed those whom all the moral lectures in the world could never have moved. Judged and condemned by the unanswerable reasonings of their own consciences, they have not had control enough over their passions to shake off the captivity in which they were held by the temptations that assailed them at every turn, till they have drawn near to the cross of Jesus, and from pardon have gathered hope, and from hope have gained strength to master sin. When they have seen their sin laid on Jesus, they have loved Him, and hated the sin that made Him to suffer so grievously as their substitute. Then the Holy Ghost has come upon them, and they have resolved, with divine strength to drive out the sin for which the Saviour died; they have begun a new life, ay, and they have continued in it, sustained by that same sacred power which first constrained them, and now they look forward to be perfected by it through the power of God.

Where are the triumphs of infidelity in rescuing men from sin? Where are the trophies of philosophy in conquering human pride? Will you bring us harlots that have been made chaste; thieves that have been reclaimed; angry men, of bear-like temper, who have become harmless as lambs, through scientific lectures? Let our amateur philanthropists, who suggest so much and do so little, produce some instances of the moral transformations that have been wrought by their sophistries. Nay; they curl their lips, and leave the lower orders to the City Missionary and the Bible Woman. It is the cross that humbles the haughty, lifts up the fallen, refines the polluted, and gives a fresh start to those who are forlorn and desperate. Nothing else can do it. The world sinks lower and lower into the bog of its own selfishness and sin. Only this wondrous lever of the atonement, symbolized by the cross of Christ, can lift our abject race to the place of virtue and honour which it ought to occupy.

II. The second cross exhibits THE WORLD CRUCIFIED. The apostle says that the world was crucified to him. What does he mean by this? He regarded the world as nailed up like a felon, and hanged upon a cross to die. Well, I suppose he means that its character was condemned. He looked out upon the world which thought so much of itself, and said, "I do not think much of thee, poor world! Thou art like a doomed malefactor."

He knew that the world had crucified its Saviour—crucified its God. It had gone to such a length of sin that it had hounded perfect innocence through the streets. Infinite benevolence it had scoffed at and maligned. Eternal truth it had rejected, and preferred a lie; and the Son of God, who was love incarnate, it had put to the death of the cross.

"Now," says Paul, "I know thy character, O world! I know thee! and I hold thee in no more esteem than the wretch abhorred for his crimes, who is condemned to hang upon the gibbet and so end his detested life." This led Paul, since he condemned its character, utterly to despise its judgment. The world said, "This Paul is a fool. His gospel is foolishness and he himself is a mere babbler." "Yes," thought Paul, "a deal you know of it!" In this we unite with him. What is your judgment worth? You did not know the Son of God, poor blind world! We are sure that He was perfect, and yet you hunted Him to death. Your judgment is a poor thing, O world! You are crucified to us.

We are told to think a great deal about "public opinion," "popular belief," "the growing feeling of the age," "the sentiment of the period," and "the spirit of the age." I should like Paul to read some of our religious newspapers; and yet I could not wish the good man so distasteful a task, for I dare say he would sooner pine in the Mammertine prison than do so; but, still, I should like to see how he would look after he had read some of those expressions about the necessity of keeping ourselves abreast with the sentiment of the period. "What," he would say, "the sentiment of the world! It is crucified to me! What can it matter what its opinion is? We are of God, little children, and the whole world lieth in the wicked one; would ye heed what the world, that is lying in the wicked one, thinks of you or of the truth of your Lord? Are you going to smooth your tongue, and soften your speech, to please the world that lieth in the wicked one!" Paul would be indignant with such a proposition. He said, "the world is crucified to me." Hence he looked upon all the world's pleasures as so much rottenness, a carcase nailed to a cross.

Can you fancy Paul being taken to the Colosseum at Rome? I try to imagine him made to sit on one of those benches to watch a combat of gladiators. There is the emperor: there are all the great peers of Rome and the senators; and there are those cruel eyes all gazing down upon men who shed each other's blood. Can you picture how Paul would have felt if he had been forced to occupy a seat at that spectacle? It would have been martyrdom to him. He would have closed his eyes and ears against the sight of what Rome thought to be the choicest pleasure of the day. They thronged the imperial city; they poured in mighty streams into the theatre each day to see poor beasts tortured, or men murdering one another: that was the world of Paul's day: and he rightly judged it to be a crucified felon. If he was compelled to see the popular pleasures of to-day, upon which I will say but little, would he not be well-nigh as sick of them as he would have been of the amusements of the amphitheatre at Rome?

To Paul, too, all the honours of the age must have been crucified in like manner. Suppose that Paul settled his mind to think of the wretches who were reigning as emperors in his day! I use the word advisedly, for I would not speak evil of dignities; but really I speak too well of them when I call them wretches. They seem to have been inhuman monsters—"tyrants whose capricious folly violated every law of nature and decency," to whom every kind of lust was a daily habit, and who even sought out new inventions of sensuality, calling them new pleasures. As Paul thought of the iniquities of Napoli, and all the great towns to which the Romans went in their holidays—Pompeii and the like—oh, how he loathed them! And I doubt not that if the apostle were to come here now, if he knew how often rank and title are wont to sink all true dignity in shameful dissipation, and what flagrant profligacy is to be found in high quarters, he might as justly consider all the pomps and dignities and honours of the world that now is to be as little worth as a putrid carcase hanging on a tree and rotting in the sun. He says, "The world is crucified to me: it is hanging on the gallows to me, I think so little of its pleasures and of its pomps."

Alike contemptuously did Paul judge of all the treasures of the world. Paul never spent as much time as it would take to wink his eye in thinking of how much money he was worth. Having food and raiment he was therewith content. Sometimes he had scarcely that. He casually thanks the Philippians for ministering to his necessities, but he never sought to store anything, nor did he live with even half a thought of aggrandizing himself with gold and silver. "No," he said, "this will all perish with the using," and so he treated the world as a thing crucified to him. Now, Christian man, can you say as much as this—that the world, in its mercantile aspect, as well as in its motley vices and its manifold frivolities, is a crucified thing to you? Now, look what the world says. "Make money, young man, make money! Honestly if you can, but by all means make money. Look about you, for if you are not sharp you will not succeed. Keep your own counsel, and rather play the double than be the dupe. Your character will rise with the credit you get on 'Change." Now, suppose that you get the money, what is the result? The net result, as I often find it, is a paragraph in one of the newspapers to say that So-and-so Esquire's will was proved in the Probate Court under so many thousands. Then follows a grand squabble among all his relatives which shall eat him up. That is the consummation of a life of toil and care and scheming. He has lived for lucre, and he has to leave it behind. There is the end of that folly.

Oh, it is a poor thing to live for, the making of money and the hoarding of it. But still the genius of rightly getting money can be consecrated to the glory of God. You can use the wealth of this world in the service of the Master. To gain is not wrong. It is only wrong when grasping becomes the main object of life, and grudging grows into covetousness which is idolatry. To every Christian that and every other form of worldliness ought to be crucified, so that we can say, "For me to live is not myself, but it is Christ; I live that I may honour and glorify Him."

When the apostle said that the world was crucified to him, he meant just this. "I am not enslaved by any of its pursuits. I care nothing for its maxims. I am not governed by its spirit. I do not court its smiles. I do not fear its threatenings. It is not my master, nor am I its slave. The whole world cannot force Paul to lie, or to sin, but Paul will tell the world the truth, come what may." You recollect the words of Palissy, the potter, when the king of France said to him that if he did not change his religion, and cease to be a Huguenot, he was afraid that he should have to deliver him up to his enemies. "Sire," said the potter, "I am sorry to hear you say, 'I am afraid,' for all the men in the world could not make Palissy talk like that. I am afraid of nobody, and I *must* do nothing but what is right." Oh, yes; the man that fears God and loves the cross has a moral backbone which enables him to stand, and he snaps his fingers at the world. "Dead felon!" says he, "dead felon! Crucifier of Christ! Cosmos thou callest thyself. By comely names thou wouldst fain be greeted. Paul is nothing in thine esteem; but Paul is a match for thee, for he thinks as much of thee as thou dost of him, and no more." Hear him as he cries, "The world is crucified unto me, and I unto the world." To live to serve men is one thing, to live to bless them is another; and this we will do, God helping us, making sacrifices for their good. But to fear men, to ask their leave to think, to ask their instructions as to what we will speak, and how we shall say it—that is a baseness we cannot brook. By the grace of God, we have not so degraded ourselves, and never shall. "The world is crucified to me," says the apostle, "by the cross of Christ."

III. Then he finishes up with the third crucifixion, which is, *I AM CRUCIFIED TO THE WORLD.* We shall soon see the evidence of

I

this crucifixion if we notice how they poured contempt upon him. Once Saul was a great rabbi, a man profoundly versed in Hebrew lore, a Pharisee of the Pharisees, and much admired. He was also a classic scholar and a philosophic thinker, a man of great mental powers, and fit to take the lead in learned circles. But when Paul began to preach Christ crucified—"Bah," they said, "he is an utter fool! Heed him not!" Or else they said, "Down with him! He is an apostate!" They cursed him. His name brought wrath unto the face of all Jews that mentioned it, and all intelligent Greeks likewise. "Paul? He is nobody!" He was everybody when he thought their way: he is nobody now that he thinks in God's way.

And then they put him to open shame by suspecting all his motives, and by misrepresenting all his actions. It did not matter what Paul did, they were quite certain that he was self-seeking; and he was endeavouring to make a fine thing of it for himself. When he acted so that they were forced to own that he was right, they put it in such a light that they made it out to be wrong. There were some who denied his apostleship, and said that he was never sent of God; and others questioned his ability to preach the gospel. So they crucified poor Paul one way and another to the full.

They went further still. They despised, they shunned him. His old friends forsook him. Some got out of the way, others pointed at him the finger of scorn in the streets. His persecutors showed their rancour against him, now stoning him with lynch-law, and anon with a semblance of legality dragging him before the magistrates. Paul was crucified to them. As for his teaching, they decried him as a babbler—a setter-forth of strange gods. I dare say they often sneered at the cross of Christ which he preached as a nine days' wonder, an almost exploded doctrine, and said, "If you do but shut the mouths of such men as Paul, it will soon be forgotten." I have heard them say in modern times to lesser men, "Your old-fashioned Puritanism is nearly dead, ere long it will be utterly extinct!" But we preach Christ crucified; the same old doctrine as the apostles preached, and for this by the contempt of the worldly wise we are crucified.

Now, dear Christian friends, if you keep to the cross of Christ you must expect to have this for your portion. The world will be crucified to you, and you will be crucified to the world. You will get the cold shoulder. Old friends will become open foes. They will begin to hate you more than they loved you before. At home your foes will be the men of your own household. You will hardly be able to do anything right. When you joined in their revels you were a fine fellow; when you could drink, and sing a lascivious song, you were a jolly good fellow; but now they rate you as a fool; they scout you as a hypocrite; and slanderously blacken your character. Let their dislike be a badge of your discipleship, and say, "Now also the world is crucified to me, and I unto the world. Whatever the world says against me for Christ's sake is the maundering of a doomed malefactor, and what do I care for that? And, on the other hand, if I be rejected and despised, I am only taking what I always expected—my crucifixion—in my poor, humble way, after the manner of Christ Himself, who was despised and rejected of men."

The moral and the lesson of it all is this. Whatever comes of it, still glory in Christ. Go in for this, dear friends, that whether ye be in honour or in dishonour, in good report or in evil report, whether God multiply your substance and make you rich, or diminish it and make you poor, you will still glory in the cross of Christ. If you have health, and strength and vigour to work for Him, or if you have to lie upon a bed of languishing and bear in patience all your heavenly Father's will, resolve that you will still glory in the cross. Let this be the point of your glorying throughout your lives. Go down the steeps of Jordan, and go through Jordan itself, still glorying in the cross, for in the heaven of glory you will find that the blood-bought hosts celebrate the cross as the trophy of their redemption.

Are you trusting in the cross? Are you resting in Jesus? If not, may the Lord teach you this blessed privilege. There is no joy like it. There is no strength like it. There is no life like it. There is no peace like it. At the cross we find our heaven. While upon the cross we gaze all heavenly, holy things abound within our hearts. If you have never been there, the Lord lead you there at this very hour; so shall you be pardoned, accepted, and blest for aye. The Lord grant that you all may be partakers of this grace for Christ's sake. Amen.

THE SHAME AND SPITTING

Text.—"I gave my back to the smiters, and my cheeks to them that plucked off the hair: I hid not my face from shame and spitting." —Isaiah l. 6.

Of whom speaketh the prophet this? Of himself or of some other? We cannot doubt but what Isaiah here wrote concerning the Lord Jesus Christ. Is not this one of the prophecies to which our Lord Himself referred in the incident recorded in the eighteenth chapter of Luke's gospel at the thirty-first verse? "Then he took unto him the twelve, and said unto them, Behold, we go up to Jerusalem, and all things that are written by the prophets concerning the Son of man shall be accomplished. For he shall be delivered unto the Gentiles, and shall be mocked, and spitefully entreated, and spitted on: and they shall scourge him, and put him to death." Such a remarkable prophecy of scourging and spitting as this which is now before us must surely refer to the Lord Jesus; its highest fulfilment is assuredly found in Him alone.

Of whom else, let me ask, could you conceive the prophet to have spoken if you read the whole chapter? Of whom else could he say in the same breath, "I clothe the heavens with blackness, and I make sackcloth their covering. I gave my back to the smiters, and my cheeks to them that plucked off the hair." (Verses 3 and 6.) What a descent from the omnipotence which veils the heavens with clouds to the gracious condescension which does not veil its own face, but permits it to be spat upon! No other could thus have spoken of Himself but He who is both God and man. He must be divine: how else could He say, "Behold, at my rebuke I dry up the sea, I make the rivers a wilderness"? (Verse 2.) And yet He must at the same time be a "Man of sorrows and acquainted with grief," for there is a strange depth of pathos in the words, "I gave my back to the smiters, and my cheeks to them that plucked off the hair: I hid not my face from shame and spitting." Whatever others may say, we believe that the speaker in this verse is Jesus of Nazareth, the King of the Jews, the Son of God and the Son of man, our Redeemer. It is the Judge of Israel whom they have smitten with a rod upon the cheek who here plaintively declares the griefs which He has undergone. We have before us the language of prophecy, but it is as accurate as though it had been written at the moment of the event. Isaiah might have been one of the Evangelists, so exactly does he describe what our Saviour endured.

It was at His third trial, when He was delivered altogether to the Gentiles, that Pilate, the governor, gave Him up to the cruel process of scourging. Scourging as it was practised in the English army was atrocious. But the lash is nothing among us compared with what it was among the Romans. I have heard that it was made of the sinews of oxen, and that in it were twisted the huckle-bones of sheep, with slivers of bone, in order that every stroke might more effectually tear its way into the poor quivering flesh, which was mangled by its awful strokes. Scourging was such a punishment that it was generally regarded as worse than death itself, and indeed, many perished while enduring it, or soon afterwards. Our blessed Redeemer gave His back to the smiters, and the ploughers made deep furrows there. O spectacle of misery! How can we bear to look thereon?

Nor was that all, for Pilate's soldiers, calling all the band together, as if there were not enough for mockery unless all were mustered, put Him to derision by a mock enthronement and a mimic coronation; and when they had thus done they again buffeted and smote Him, and spat in His face. There was no kind of cruelty which their heartlessness could just then invent which they did not exercise upon His blessed person: their brutal sport had full indulgence, for their innocent victim offered neither resistance nor remonstrance. This is His own record of His patient endurance, "I gave my back to the smiters, and my cheeks to them that plucked off the hair: I hid not my face from shame and spitting."

Behold your King! I bring Him forth to you this morning in spirit and cry, "Behold the Man!" Turn hither all your eyes and hearts and look upon the despised and rejected of men! Gaze reverently and lovingly, with awe for His sufferings and love for His person. The sight demands adoration. I would remind you of that which Moses did when he saw the bush that burned and was not consumed—fit emblem of our Lord on fire with griefs and yet not destroyed; I bid you turn aside and see this great sight, but first attend to the mandate—"put off thy shoes from off thy feet, for the place whereon thou standest is holy ground." All round the cross the soil is sacred. Our suffering Lord has consecrated every place whereon He stood, and therefore our hearts must be filled with reverence while we linger under the shadow of His passion.

May the Holy Spirit help you to see Jesus in four lights at this time. In each view He is worthy of devout attention. Let us view Him first as *the representative of God*; secondly, as *the substitute of His people*; thirdly, as *the servant of Jehovah*; and fourthly, as *the Comforter of His redeemed*.

I. First, I invite you to gaze upon your despised and rejected Lord as THE REPRESENTATIVE OF GOD. In the person of Christ Jesus, God Himself came into the world, making a special visitation to Jerusalem and the Jewish people, but at the same time coming very near to all mankind. The Lord called to the people whom He had favoured so long and whom He was intent to favour still. He says, in the second verse, "I came" and "I called." God did in very deed come down into the midst of mankind.

Be it noted, that when our Lord came into this world as the representative of God, He came with all His divine power about Him. The chapter before us says, "Is my hand shortened at all, that it cannot redeem? or have I no power to deliver? behold, at my rebuke I dry up the sea, I make the rivers a wilderness." The Son of God, when He was here, did not perform those exact miracles, because He was bent upon marvels of beneficence rather than of judgment. He did not repeat the plagues of Egypt, for He did not come to smite, but to save; but He did greater wonders and wrought miracles which ought far more powerfully to have won men's confidence in Him because they were full of goodness and mercy. He fed the hungry, He healed the sick, He raised the dead, and He cast out devils. He did equal marvels to those which were wrought in Egypt when the arm of the Lord was made bare in the eyes of all the people. It is true He did not change water into blood, but He turned water into wine. It is true He did not make their fish to stink, but by His word He caused the net to be filled even to bursting with great fishes. He did not break the whole staff of bread as He did in Egypt, but He multiplied loaves and fishes so that thousands of men and women and children were fed from His bounteous hand. He did not slay their firstborn, but He restored the dead.

I grant you that the glory of the Godhead was somewhat hidden in the person of Jesus of Nazareth, but it was still there, even as the glory was upon the face of Moses when he covered it with a veil. No essential attribute of God was absent in Christ, and every one might have been seen in Him if the people had not been wilfully blind. He did the works of His Father, and those works bear witness of Him that He was come in His Father's name. Yes, God was personally in the world when Jesus walked the blessed fields of the Holy Land, now, alas, laid under the curse for rejecting Him.

But when God thus came among men He was unacknowledged. What saith the prophet? "Wherefore when I came was there no man? when I called was there none to answer?" A few, taught by the Spirit of God, discerned Him and rejoiced; but they were so very few that we may say of the whole generation that they knew Him not. Those who had some dim idea of His excellence and majesty yet rejected Him. Herod, because he feared that He was a king, sought to slay Him. The kings of the earth set themselves, and the rulers took counsel together, against the Lord, and against His anointed. He was emphatically and beyond all others "despised and rejected of men." Though, as I have said, the Godhead in Him was but scantily veiled, and gleams of its glory burst forth ever and anon, yet still the people would have none of it, and the cry, "Away with him, away with him, let him be crucified," was the verdict of the age upon which He descended. He called and there was none to answer; He spread out His hands all the day long unto a rebellious people who utterly rejected Him.

Yet our Lord when He came into the world was admirably adapted to be the representative of God, not only because He was God Himself, but because as man His whole nature was consecrated to the work, and in Him was neither flaw nor spot. He was untouched by any motive other than the one desire of manifesting the Father and blessing the sons of men. Oh, beloved, there was never one who had his ear so near the mouth of God as Jesus had. His Father had no need to speak to Him in dreams and visions of the night, for when all His faculties were wide awake there was nothing in them to hinder His understanding the mind of God; and therefore every morning when His Father wakened Him He spake into His ear. Jesus sat as a scholar at the Father's feet that He might learn first, and then teach. The things which He heard of the Father He made known unto men. He says that He spake not His own words but the words of Him that sent Him, and He did not His own deeds, but "my Father," said He, "that dwelleth in me, he doeth the work."

His errand, too, was all gentleness and love, for He came to speak words in season to the weary, and to comfort those that were cast down: surely such an errand should have secured Him a welcome. His course and conduct were most conciliatory, for He went among the people, and ate with publicans and sinners; so gentle was He that He took little children in His arms, and blessed them; for this, if for nothing else, they ought to have welcomed Him right heartily and rejoiced at the sight of Him. Our text tells us how contrary was their conduct towards Him to that which He deserved: instead of being welcomed He was scourged, and instead of being honoured He was scorned. Cruelty smote His back and plucked off the hair from His face, while derision jeered at Him and cast its spittle upon Him. Shame and contempt were poured upon Him, though He was God Himself. That spectacle of Christ spat upon, and scourged, represents what man virtually does to his God, what he would do to the Most High if he could. Hart well puts it:—

> "See how the patient Jesus stands,
> Insulted in His lowest case!
> Sinners have bound the Almighty hands,
> And spit in their Creator's face."

When our parents broke the command of their Maker, obeying the advice of the devil rather than the word of God, and preferring a poor apple to the divine favour, they did as it were spit into the face of God; and every sin committed since has been a repetition of the same contempt of the Eternal One. When a man will have his pleasure, even though it displeases God, he as good as declares that he despises God, prefers himself, and defies the wrath of the Most High. When a man acts contrary to the command of God he does as good as say to God, "This is better for me to do than what Thou bidst me do. Either Thou art mistaken, in Thy prohibitions, or else Thou dost wilfully deny me the highest pleasure, and I, being a better judge of my own interests than Thou art, snatch at the pleasure which Thou dost refuse me. I judge Thee either to be unwise or unkind." Every act of sin does despite to the sovereignty of God: it denies Him to be supreme, and refuses Him obedience. Every act of sin does dishonour to the love and wisdom of God, for it seems to say that it would have been greater love to have permitted us to do evil than to have commanded us to abstain from it. All sin is in many ways an insult to the majesty of the thrice Holy God, and He regards it as such.

Dear friends, this is especially the sin of those who have heard the gospel and yet reject the Saviour, for in their case the Lord has come to them in the most gracious form, and yet they have refused Him. The Lord might well say, "I have come to you to save you, and you will not regard me. I have come saying to you, 'Look unto me and be ye saved, all the ends of the earth,' and you close your eyes in unbelief. I have come saying, 'Let us reason together: though your sins be as crimson, they shall be as wool,' but you will not be cleansed from your iniquity. I have come with the promise, 'All manner of sin and iniquity shall be forgiven unto men.' What is your reply?" In the case of many the answer is, "We prefer our own righteousness to the righteousness of God." If that is not casting spittle into the face of God I know not what is, for our righteousnesses are well described as "filthy rags," and we have the impudence to say that these are better than the righteousness of God in Christ Jesus.

Or if we do not say this when we reject the Saviour we tell Him that we do not want Him, for we do not need a Saviour: this is as good as to say that God has played the fool with the life and death of His own Son. What greater derision can be cast upon God than to consider the blood of atonement to be a superfluity? He who chooses sin sooner than repentance prefers to suffer the wrath of God rather than be holy and dwell in heaven for ever. For the sake of a few paltry pleasures men forego the love of God, and are ready to run the risk of an eternity of divine wrath. They think so little of God that He is of no account with them at all. All this is in reality a scorning and despising of the Lord God, and is well set forth by the insults which were poured upon the Lord Jesus.

Woe's me that it should ever be so. My God! my God! To what a sinful race do I belong. Alas, that it should treat Thine infinite goodness so despitefully! That Thou shouldst be rejected at all, but especially that thou shouldest be rejected when dressed in robes of love and arrayed in gentleness and pity is horrible to think upon. But there is the picture before you. God Himself set at nought, despised, rejected, put to shame, perpetually dishonoured in the person of His dear Son. The sight should breed repentance in us. We should look to Him whom we have scourged, and mourn for Him. O Holy Spirit, work this tender grace in all our hearts.

II. And now, secondly, I want to set the Lord Jesus before you in another light, or rather beseech Him to shine in His own light before your eyes:—AS THE SUBSTITUTE FOR HIS PEOPLE. Recollect when our Lord Jesus Christ suffered thus it was not on His own account nor purely for the sake of His Father, but He "was wounded for our transgressions, he was bruised for our iniquities: the chastisement of our peace was upon him; and with his stripes we are healed." There has risen up a modern idea which I cannot too much reprobate, that Christ made no atonement for our sin except upon the cross: whereas in this passage of Isaiah we are taught as plainly as possible that by His bruising and His stripes, as well as by His death, we are healed. Never divide between the life and the death of Christ. How could He have died if He had not lived? How could He suffer except while He lived? Death is not suffering, but the end of it. Guard also against the evil notion that you have nothing to do with the righteousness of Christ, for He could not have made an atonement by His blood if He had not been perfect in His life. He could not have been acceptable if He had not first been proven to be holy, harmless, and undefiled. The victim must be spotless, or it cannot be presented for sacrifice. Draw no nice lines and raise no quibbling questions, but look at your Lord as He is and bow before Him.

Understand, my dear brothers and sisters, that Jesus took upon Himself our sin, and being found bearing that sin He had to be treated as sin should be treated. Now, of all the things that ever existed sin is the most shameful thing that can be. It deserves to be scourged, it deserves to be spit upon, it deserves to be crucified; and because our Lord had taken upon Himself our sin, therefore must He be put to shame, therefore must He be scourged. If you want to see what God thinks of sin, see His only Son spat upon by the soldiers when He was made sin for us. In God's sight sin is a shameful, horrible, loathsome, abominable thing, and when Jesus takes it He must be forsaken and given up to scorn. This sight will be the more wonderful to you when you recollect who it was that was spat upon, for if you and I, being sinners, were scourged, and smitten, and despised, there would be no wonder in it; but He who took our sin was God, before whom angels bow with reverent awe, and yet, seeing the sin was upon Him, He was made subject to the most intense degree of shame. Seeing that Jesus stood in our stead, it is written of the eternal Father that "He spared not his own Son." "It pleased the Father to bruise him: he hath put him to grief"; He made His soul an offering for sin. Yes, beloved, sin is condemned in the flesh and made to appear exceeding shameful when you recollect that, even though it was only laid on our blessed Lord by imputation, yet it threw Him into the very depths of shame and woe ere it could be removed.

Reflect, also, upon the voluntariness of all this. He willingly submitted to the endurance of suffering and scorn. It is said in the text, "He *gave* his back to the smiters." They did not seize and compel Him, or, if they did, yet they could not have done it without His consent. He gave His back to the smiters. He gave His cheek to those that plucked off the hair. He did not hide His face from shame and spitting: He did not seek in any way to escape from insults. It was the voluntariness of His grief which constituted in great measure the merit of it. That Christ should stand in our stead by force were a little thing, even had it been possible; but that He should stand there of His own free will, and that being there He should willingly be treated with derision, this is grace indeed. The Son of God was willingly made a curse for us, and at His own desire was made subject to shame on our account.

I do not know how you feel in listening to me, but while I am speaking I feel as if language ought scarcely to touch such a theme as this: it is too feeble for its task. I want you to get beyond my words if you can, and for yourselves meditate upon the fact that He who covers the heavens with blackness, yet did not cover His own face, and He who binds up the universe with the girdle which holds it in one, yet was bound and blindfolded by the men He had Himself made; He whose face is as the brightness of the sun that shineth in its strength was once spit upon. Surely we shall need faith in heaven to believe this wondrous fact. Can it have been true, that the glorious Son of God was jeered and jested at?

I have often heard that there is no faith wanted in heaven, but I rather judge that we shall want as much faith to believe that these things were ever done as the patriarchs had to believe that they would be done. How shall I sit down and gaze upon *Him* and think that His dear face was once profaned with spittle? When all heaven shall lie prostrate at His feet in awful silence of adoration will it seem possible that once He was mocked? When angels, and principalities, and powers shall all be roused to rapture of harmonious music in His praise, will it seem possible that once the most abject of men plucked out the hair? Will it not appear incredible that those sacred hands, which are "as gold rings set with the beryl," were once nailed to a gibbet, and that those cheeks which are "as a bed of spices, as sweet flowers," should have been battered and bruised? We shall be quite certain of the fact, and yet we shall never cease to wonder, that His side was gashed, and His face was spit upon? The sin of man in this instance will always amaze us. How could you commit this crime? Oh, ye sons of men, how could ye treat such a one with cruel scorn? O thou brazen thing called sin. Thou hast, indeed, as the prophet saith, "A whore's forehead"; thou hast a demon's heart, hell burns within thee. Why couldst thou not spit upon earthly splendours? Why must heaven be thy scorn? Or if heaven, why not spit on angels: Was there no place for thy base deed but the Well-beloved's face? Was there no place for thy spittle but *His* face? *His* face! Woe is me! His face! Should such loveliness receive such shame as this? I could wish that man had never been created, or that, being created, he had been swept into nothingness rather than have lived to commit such horror.

Yet here is matter for our faith to rest upon. Beloved, trust yourselves in the hands of your great Substitute. Did He bear all this shame? then there must be more than enough merit and efficacy in this, which was the prelude of His precious death —and especially in His death itself—there must be merit sufficient to put away all transgression, iniquity, and sin. Our shame is ended, for He has borne it! Our punishment is removed: He has endured it all. Double for all our sins has our Redeemer paid. Return unto thy rest, O my soul, and let peace take full possession of thy weeping heart.

III. But time fails us, and therefore we will mention, next, the third light in which it is our desire to see the Saviour. Beloved, we desire to see the Lord Jesus Christ AS THE SERVANT OF GOD. He took upon Himself the form of a servant when He was made in the likeness of man. Observe how He performed this service right thoroughly, and remember we are to look upon this third picture as our copy, which is to be the guide of our life. I know that many of you are glad to call yourselves the servants of God; take not the name in vain. As Jesus was, so are you also in this world, and you are to seek to be like Him.

First, as a servant, Christ was personally prepared for service. He was thirty years and more here below, learning obedience in His Father's house, and the after years were spent in learning obedience by the things which He suffered. What a servant He was, for He never went about His own errands nor went by His own will, but He waited always upon His Father. He was in constant communication with heaven, both by day and by night. He says, "He wakeneth morning by morning, he wakeneth mine ear to hear as the learned." The blessed Lord or ever the day broke heard that gentle voice which called Him, and at its whisper He arose before the sunrise, and there the dawning found Him, on the mountain side, waiting upon God in wrestling prayer, taking His message from the Father that He might go and deliver it to the children of men. He loved man much, but He loved His Father more, and He never came to tell out the love of God without having as man received it fresh from the divine heart. He knew that His Father heard Him always, and He lived in the spirit of conscious acceptance.

Our text assures us that this service knew no reserve in its consecration. *We* generally draw back somewhere. I am ashamed to say it, but I mourn that I have done so. Many of us could give to Christ all our health and strength, and all the money we have, very heartily and cheerfully; but when it comes to a point of reputation we feel the pinch. To be slandered, to have some filthy thing said of you; this is too much for flesh and blood. You seem to say, "I cannot be made a fool of, I cannot bear to be regarded as a mere imposter"; but a true servant of Christ must make himself of no reputation when he takes upon himself the work of his Lord. Our blessed Master was willing to be scoffed at by the lewdest and the lowest of men. The abjects jeered at Him; the reproach of them that reproached God fell upon Him. He became the song of the drunkard, and when the rough soldiery detained Him in the guard-room they heaped up their ridicule, as though He were not worthy of the name of man.

"They bow their knees to Me, and cry, 'Hail, King':
Whatever scoffs or scornfulness can bring,
I am the floor, the sink, where they it fling:
Was ever grief like Mine?

"The soldiers also spit upon that face
Which angels did desire to have the grace
And prophets once to see, but found no place:
Was ever grief like Mine?"

Herod and Pilate were the very dross of men, and yet He permitted them to judge Him. Their servants were vile fellows, and yet He resigned Himself to them. If he had breathed upon them with angry breath, He might have flashed devouring fire upon them, and burned them up as stubble; but His omnipotent patience restrained His indignation, and He remained as a sheep before her shearers. He allowed His own creatures to pluck His hair and spit in His face. Such patience should be yours as servants of God. We are to be willing to be made nothing of, and even to be counted as the offscouring of all things. It is pitiful for the Christian to refuse to suffer, and to become a fighting man, crying, "We must stand up for our rights." Did you ever see Jesus in that posture? There is a propensity in us to say, "I will have it out." Yes, but you cannot picture Jesus in that attitude. I defy a painter to depict Him so: it is somebody else, and not Christ. No! He said, "I gave my back to the smiters, and my cheeks to them that plucked off the hair: I hid not my face from shame and spitting."

All this while—now follow me in this next point—there was no flinching in Him. They spat in His face, but what says He in the seventh verse. "I have set my face like a flint." If they are about to defile His face He is resolved to bear it; He girds up His loins, and makes Himself more determined. Oh, the bravery of our Master's silence! Cruelty and shame could not make Him speak. Have not your lips sometimes longed to speak out a denial and a defence? Have you not felt it wise to be quiet, but then the charge has been so excessively cruel, and it has stung you so terribly that you hungered to resent it. Base falsehoods aroused your indignation, and you felt you must speak and probably you did speak, though you tried to keep your lips as with a bridle while the wicked were before you. But our own beloved Lord in the omnipotence of His patience and love would

not utter a word, but like a lamb at the slaughter He opened
not His mouth. He witnessed a good confession by His matchless silence. Oh, how mighty—how gloriously mighty was His
patience! We must copy it if we are to be His disciples. We,
too, must set our faces like flints, to move or to sit still, according
to the Father's will, to be silent or to speak, as most shall honour
Him. "I have set my face like a flint," saith He, even though
in another place He cries, "My heart is like wax, it is melted in
the midst of my bowels."

And do you notice all the while the confidence and quiet
of His spirit? He almost seems to say, "You may spit upon Me,
but you cannot find fault with Me. You may pluck My hair, but
you cannot impugn My integrity; you may lash My shoulders,
but you cannot impute a fault to Me. Your false witnesses dare
not look Me in the face: let Me know who is Mine adversary,
let him come near to Me. Behold, Adonai Jehovah will keep Me,
who is he that shall condemn Me! Lo, they all shall wax old
as a garment, the moth shall eat them up." Be calm then, O
true servant of God! In patience possess your soul. Serve God
steadily and steadfastly though all men should belie you. Go to
the bottom of the service, dive even to the very depth, and be
content even to lie in Christ's grave, for you shall share in Christ's
resurrection. Do not dream that the path to heaven is up the
hill of honour, it winds down into the valley of humiliation.
Imagine not that you can grow great eternally by being great
here. You must become less, and less, and less, even though
you should be despised and rejected of men, for this is the path
to everlasting glory.

IV. Lastly, I am to set Him forth in His fourth character, as
THE COMFORTER OF HIS PEOPLE; but I must ask *you* to do this,
while I just, as it were, make a charcoal sketch of the picture
I would have painted.

Remember, first, our blessed Lord is well qualified to speak
a word in season to him that is weary, because He Himself is
lowly, and meek, and so accessible to us. When men are in
low spirits they feel as if they could not take comfort from persons
who are harsh and proud. The comforter must come as a sufferer;
He must come in a lowly, broken spirit, if He would cheer the
afflicted. You must not put on your best dress to go and visit
the daughter of poverty, or go with your jewels about you to
show how much better off you are than she. Sit down by the
side of the downcast man and let him know that you are meek
and lowly of heart. Your Master "gave his back to the smiters,
and his cheek to them that plucked off the hair," and therefore
He is the Comforter you want.

Remark not only His lowliness, but His sympathy. Are you

full of aches and pains this morning? Jesus knows all about them, for He "gave his back to the smiters." Do you suffer from what is worse than pain, from scandal and slander? "He hid not his face from shame and spitting." Have you been ridiculed of late? Have the graceless made fun of your godliness? Jesus can sympathise with you, for you know what unholy mirth they made out of Him. In every pang that rends your heart your Lord has borne His share. Go and tell Him. Many will not understand you. You are a speckled bird, differing from all the rest, and they will all peck at you; but Jesus Christ knows this, for He was a speckled bird too. He was "holy, harmless, undefiled, and separate from sinners," but not separate from such as you. Get you to Him and He will sympathise with you.

In addition to His gentle spirit and His power to sympathise, there is this to help to comfort us—namely, His example, for He can argue thus with you, "I gave my back to the smiters. Cannot you do the like? Shall the disciple be above his master?" If I can but get on the doorstep of heaven and sit down in the meanest place there I shall feel I have an infinitely better position than I deserve, and shall I think of my dear, blessed Lord and Master giving His face to be spit upon, and then give myself airs, and say, "I cannot bear this scorn, I cannot bear this pain!" What, does the King pass over the brook Kedron, and must there be no brook Kedron for you? Does the Master bear the cross, and must your shoulders never be galled? Did they call the Master of the house "Beelzebub," and must they call you "Reverend Sir?" Did they laugh at Him, and scoff at Him, and must you be honoured? Are you to be "gentleman" and "lady" where Christ was "that fellow"? For His birth they loaned Him a stable, and for His burial He borrowed a grave. O, friends, let pride disappear, and let us count it our highest honour to be permitted to stoop as low as ever we can.

And, then, His example further comforts us by the fact that He was calm amid it all. Oh, the deep rest of the Saviour's heart! They set Him up upon that mock throne, but He did not answer with an angry word; they put a reed into His hand, but He did not change it to an iron rod, and break them like potter's vessel, as He might have done. There was no wincing and no pleading for mercy. Sighs of pain were forced from Him, and He said, "I thirst," for He was not a stoic; but there was no fear of man, or timorous shrinking of heart.

The King of Martyrs well deserves to wear the martyr's crown, for right royally did He endure: there was never a patience like to His. That is your copy, brother, that is your copy, sister— you must write very carefully to write as well as that. You had need your Master held your hand; in fact, whenever children in Christ's school do write according to His copy, it is always because He holds their hand by His Spirit.

Last of all, our Saviour's triumph is meant to be a stimulus and encouragement to us. He stands before us this morning as the Comforter of His people. Consider Him that endured such contradiction of sinners against Himself lest ye be weary and faint in your minds; for though He was once abased and despised, yet now He sitteth at the right hand of God, and reigns over all things; and the day is coming when every knee shall bow before Him, and every tongue confess that Jesus Christ is Lord, to the glory of God the Father. They that spat upon Him will rue the day. Come hither, ye that derided Him! He has raised you from the dead, come hither and spit upon Him now! Ye that scourged Him, bring your rods, see what ye can do in this day of His glory! See, they fly before Him, they invoke the hills to shelter them, they ask the rocks to open and conceal them. Yet it is nothing but His face, that selfsame face they spat upon, which is making earth and heaven to flee away. Yea, all things flee before the majesty of His frown who once gave His back to the smiters, and His cheeks to them that plucked off the hair. Be like Him, then, ye who bear His name; trust Him, and live for Him, and you shall reign with Him in glory for ever and ever. Amen.

THE CROSS OUR GLORY

A Sermon

Text.—"But God forbid that I should glory, save in the cross of our Lord Jesus Christ, by whom the world is crucified unto me, and I unto the world."—Galatians vi. 14.

ALMOST all men have something wherein to glory. Every bird has its own note of song. It is a poor heart that never rejoices; it is a dull packhorse that is altogether without bells. Men usually rejoice in something or other, and many men so rejoice in that which they choose that they become boastful and full of vain glory. It is very sad that men should be ruined by their glory; and yet many are so. Many glory in their shame, and more glory in that which is mere emptiness. Some glory in their physical strength, in which an ox excels them; or in their gold, which is but thick clay; or in their gifts, which are but talents with which they are entrusted. The pounds entrusted to their stewardship are thought by men to belong to themselves, and therefore they rob God of the glory of them.

O my hearers, hear ye the voice of wisdom, which crieth, "He that glorieth, let him glory only in the Lord." To live for personal glory is to be dead while we live. Be not so foolish as to perish for a bubble. Many a man has thrown his soul away for a little honour, or for the transient satisfaction of success in trifles. O men, your tendency is to glory in somewhat; your wisdom will be to find a glory worthy of an immortal mind.

The Apostle Paul had a rich choice of things in which he could have gloried. If it had been his mind to have remained among his own people, he might have been one of their most honoured rabbis. He saith in his Epistle to the Philippians, in the third chapter, "If any other man thinketh that he hath whereof he might trust in the flesh, I more: circumcised the eighth day, of the stock of Israel, of the tribe of Benjamin, an Hebrew of the Hebrews; as touching the law, a Pharisee; concerning zeal, persecuting the church; touching the righteousness which is in the law, blameless." He says that he profited in the Jews' religion above many, his equals in his own nation; and he stood high in the esteem of his fellow-professors. But when he was converted to the faith of the Lord Jesus, he said, "What things were gain to me, those I counted loss for Christ. Yea, doubtless, and I count all things but loss for the excellency of the knowledge of Christ Jesus my Lord." As soon as he was converted he forsook all glorying in his former religion and zeal, and cried, "God forbid that I should glory in my birth, my education, my proficiency in Scripture, or my regard to orthodox ritual. God forbid that I should glory, save in the cross of our Lord Jesus Christ."

Paul might also, if he had so chosen, have gloried in his sufferings for the cross of Christ; for he had been a living martyr, a perpetual self-sacrifice to the cause of the Crucified. He says, "Are they ministers of Christ? (I speak as a fool) I am more; in labours more abundant, in stripes above measure, in prisons more frequent, in deaths oft. Of the Jews five times received I forty stripes save one. Thrice was I beaten with rods, once was I stoned, thrice I suffered shipwreck, a night and a day I have been in the deep; in journeyings often, in perils of waters, in perils of robbers, in perils by mine own countrymen, in perils by the heathen, in perils in the city, in perils in the wilderness, in perils in the sea, in perils among false brethren; in weariness and painfulness, in watchings often, in hunger and thirst, in fastings often, in cold and nakedness." He was once driven to give a summary of these sufferings to establish his apostleship; but before he did so he wrote, "Would to God ye could bear with me a little in my folly." In his heart he was saying all the while, "God forbid that I should glory, save in the cross of our Lord Jesus Christ."

The great apostle had yet another reason for glorying, if he had chosen to do so; for he could speak of visions and revelations of the Lord. He says, "I knew a man in Christ above fourteen years ago, . . . caught up to the third heaven. And I knew such a man . . . how that he was caught up into Paradise, and heard unspeakable words, which it is now lawful for a man to utter." He was in danger of being exalted above measure by reason of the abundance of these revelations and hence he was humbled by a painful thorn in the flesh. Paul, when hard driven by the necessity to maintain his position in the Corinthian church, was forced to mention these things; but he liked not such glorying, he was most at ease when he said, "God forbid that I should glory, save in the cross of our Lord Jesus Christ."

Brethren, notice that Paul does not here say that he gloried in Christ, though he did so with all his heart; but he declares that he gloried most in "the cross of our Lord Jesus Christ," which in the eyes of men was the very lowest and most inglorious part of the history of the Lord Jesus. He could have gloried in the incarnation: angels sang of it, wise men came from the Far East to behold it. Did not the new-born King awake the song from heaven of "Glory to God in the highest"? He might have gloried in the life of Christ: was there ever such another, so benevolent and blameless? He might have gloried in the resurrection of Christ: it is the world's great hope concerning those that are asleep. He might have gloried in our Lord's ascension; for He "led captivity captive," and all His followers glory in His victory. He might have gloried in His Second Advent, and I doubt not that he did; for the Lord shall soon descend from heaven with a shout, with the voice of the archangel and the trump of God, to be admired in all them that believe.

Yet the apostle selected beyond all these that centre of the Christian system, that point which is most assailed by its foes, that focus of the world's derision—the cross; and, putting all else somewhat into the shade, he exclaims, "God forbid that I should glory, save in the cross of our Lord Jesus Christ." Learn, then, that the highest glory of our holy religion is the cross. The history of grace begins earlier and goes on later, but in its middle point stands the cross. Of two eternities this is the hinge; of past decrees and future glories this is the pivot. Let us come to the cross this morning, and think of it, till each one of us, in the power of the Spirit of God, shall say, "God forbid that I should glory, save in the cross of our Lord Jesus Christ."

I. First, as the Lord shall help me (for who shall describe the cross without the help of Him that did hang upon it?) WHAT DID PAUL MEAN BY THE CROSS? Did he not include under this term, first, the fact of the cross: secondly, the doctrine of the cross: and thirdly, the cross of the doctrine?

I think he meant, first of all, *the fact of the cross.* Our Lord Jesus Christ did really die upon a gibbet, the death of a felon. He was literally put to death upon a tree, accursed in the esteem of men. I beg you to notice how the apostle puts it—"the cross of our Lord Jesus Christ." In his epistles he sometimes saith "Christ," at another time "Jesus," frequently "Lord," oftentimes "our Lord"; but here he saith "our Lord Jesus Christ." There is a sort of pomp of words in this full description, as if in contrast to the shame of the cross. The terms are intended in some small measure to express the dignity of Him who was put to so ignominious a death. He is Christ the anointed, and Jesus the Saviour; He is the Lord, the Lord of all, and He is "our Lord Jesus Christ." He is not a Lord without subjects, for He *is* "our Lord"; nor is He a Saviour without saved ones, for He is "our Lord Jesus"; nor has He the anointing for Himself alone, for all of us have a share in Him as "our Christ"; in all He is ours, and was so upon the cross.

But next, I said that Paul gloried in *the doctrine of the cross*; and it was so. What is that doctrine of the cross, of which it is written that it is "to them that perish foolishness, but unto us who are saved it is the power of God and the wisdom of God"? In one word, it is the doctrine of the atonement, the doctrine that the Lord Jesus Christ was made sin for us, that Christ was once offered to bear the sins of many, and that God hath set Him forth to be the propitiation for our sins. Paul saith, "When we were yet without strength, in due time Christ died for the ungodly"; and again, "Now once in the end of the world hath he appeared to put away sin by the sacrifice of himself." The doctrine of the cross is that of sacrifice for sin: Jesus is "the Lamb of God that taketh away the sin of the world." "God so loved the world, that he gave his only-begotten Son, that whosoever believeth in him should not perish, but have everlasting life."

The doctrine is that of a full atonement made, and the utmost ransom paid. "Christ hath redeemed us from the curse of the law, being made a curse for us: for it is written, Cursed is every one that hangeth on a tree." In Christ upon the cross we see the Just dying for the unjust, that He might bring us to God; the innocent bearing the crimes of the guilty, that they might be forgiven and accepted. That is the doctrine of the cross, of which Paul was never ashamed.

This also is a necessary part of the doctrine: that whosoever believeth in Him is justified from all sin; that whosoever trusts in the Lord Jesus Christ is in that moment forgiven, justified, and accepted in the Beloved. "As Moses lifted up the serpent in the wilderness, even so must the Son of man be lifted up; that whosoever believeth in him should not perish, but have eternal life." Paul's doctrine was, "It is not of him that willeth nor of him that runneth, but of God that showeth mercy"; and it was His constant teaching that salvation is not of doings, nor of ceremonies, but simply and alone by believing in Jesus. We are to accept by an act of trust that righteousness which is already finished and completed by the death of our blessed Lord upon the cross. He who does not preach atonement by the blood of Jesus does not preach the cross; and he who does not declare justification by faith in Christ Jesus has missed the mark altogether.

But the apostle also gloried in *the cross of the doctrine*, for the death of the Son of God upon the cross is the *crux* of Christianity. Here is the difficulty, the stumbling block, and rock of offence. The Jew could not endure a crucified Messiah: he looked for pomp and power. Multitudinous ceremonies and divers washings and sacrifices, were these all to be put away and nothing left but a bleeding Saviour? At the mention of the cross the philosophic Greek thought himself insulted, and vilified the preacher as a fool. In effect he said, "You are not a man of thought and intellect; you are not abreast of the times, but are sticking in the mire of antiquated prophecies. Why not advance with the discoveries of modern thought?" The apostle, teaching a simple fact which a child might comprehend, found in it the wisdom of God. Christ upon the cross working out the salvation of men was more to him than all the sayings of the sages. As for the Roman, he would give no heed to any glorying in a dead Jew, a crucified Jew! Crushing the world beneath his iron heel, he declared that such romancing should never win him from the gods of his fathers. Paul did not blench before the sharp and practical reply of the conquerors of the world. He trembled not before Nero in his place. Whether to Greek or Jew, Roman or barbarian, bond or free, he was not ashamed of the gospel of Christ, but gloried in the cross. He had the cross for his philosophy, the cross for his tradition, the cross for his gospel, the cross for his glory, and nothing else.

II. But, secondly, WHY DID PAUL GLORY IN THE CROSS? He did not do so because he was in want of a theme; for, as I have shown you, he had a wide field for boasting if he had chosen to occupy it. He gloried in the cross from solemn and deliberate choice. He had counted the cost, he had surveyed the whole range of subjects with eagle eye, and he knew what he did, and why he did it. He was master of the art of thinking. As a metaphysician, none could excel him; as a logical thinker, none could have gone beyond him. He stands almost alone in the early Christian church, as a master mind. Others may have been more poetic, or more simple, but none were more thoughtful or argumentative than he. With decision and firmness Paul sets aside everything else, and definitely declares, throughout his whole life, "I glory in the cross." He does this exclusively, saying, "God forbid that I should glory, save in the cross."

> "Forbid it, Lord, that I should boast,
> Save in the death of Christ, my God;
> All the vain things that charm me most,
> I sacrifice them to His blood."

He would have called God to witness that he knew no ambition save that of bringing glory to the cross of Christ. As I think of this I am ready to say, "Amen" to Paul, and bid you sing that stirring verse

> "It is the old cross still,
> Hallelujah! hallelujah!
> Its triumphs let us tell,
> Hallelujah! hallelujah!

The grace of God here shone
Through Christ, the blessed Son,
Who did for sin atone;
    Hallelujah for the cross!"

Why did Paul thus glory in the cross? You may well desire
to know, for there are many nowadays who do not glory in it
but forsake it. Alas that it should be so! but there are ministers
who ignore the atonement; they conceal the cross, or say but
little about it. You may go through service after service, and
scarce hear a mention of the atoning blood; but Paul was always
bringing forward the expiation for sin: Paul never tried to explain
it away. Oh the numbers of books that have been written to
prove that the cross means an example of self-sacrifice; as if
every martyrdom did not mean that. They cannot endure a
real substitutionary sacrifice for human guilt, and an effectual
purgation of sin by the death of the great substitute. Yet the
cross means that or nothing.

I take it that this was so, first, because Paul saw in the cross
a vindication of divine justice. Where else can the justice of God
be seen so clearly as in the death of God Himself, in the person
of His dear Son? If the Lord Himself suffers on account of
broken law, then is the majesty of the law honoured to the full.
Some time ago, a judge in America was called upon to try a
prisoner who had been his companion in his early youth. It was
a crime for which the penalty was a fine, more or less heavy.
The judge did not diminish the fine; the case was clearly a bad
one, and he fined the prisoner to the full. Some who knew the
former relation to the offender thought him somewhat unkind
thus to carry out the law, while others admired his impartiality.
All were surprised when the judge quitted the bench and himself
paid every farthing of the penalty. He had both shown his
respect for the law and his goodwill to the man who had broken
it; he exacted the penalty, but he paid it himself.

So God hath done in the Person of His dear Son. He has
not remitted the punishment, but He has Himself endured it.
His own Son, who is none other than God Himself—for there is
an essential union between them—has paid the debt which was
incurred by human sin. I love to think of the vindication of
divine justice upon the cross; I am never weary of it. Some cannot bear the thought; but to me it seems inevitable that sin must
be punished, or else the foundations of society would be removed.
If sin becomes a trifle, virtue will be a toy. Society cannot stand
if laws are left without penal sanction, or if that sanction is to
be a mere empty threat. Men in their own governments every
now and then cry out for greater severity. When a certain
offence abounds, and ordinary means fail, they demand exemplary

punishment; and it is but natural that they should do so; for deep in the conscience of every man there is the conviction thát sin must be punished to secure the general good. Justice must reign, even benevolence demands it. If there could have been salvation without an atonement it would have been a calamity; righteous men, and even benevolent men, might deprecate the setting aside of law in order to save the guilty from the natural result of their crimes.

For my own part I value a just salvation: an unjust salvation would never have satisfied the apprehensions and demands of my conscience. No, let God be just, if the heavens fall; let God carry out the sentence of His law, or the universe will suspect that it was not righteous; and when such a suspicion rules the general mind, all respect for God will be gone. The Lord carries out the decree of His justice even to the bitter end, abating not a jot of its requirements. Brethren, there was an infinite efficacy in the death of such a one as our Lord Jesus Christ to vindicate the law. Though He is Man, yet is He also God; and in His passion and death He offered to the justice of God a vindication not at all inferior to the punishment of hell. God is just indeed when Jesus dies upon the cross rather than that God's law should be dishonoured. When our august Lord Himself bore the wrath that was due for human sin, it was made evident to all that law is not to be trifled with. We glory in the cross, for there the debt was paid, our sins on Jesus laid.

But we glory because on the cross we have an unexampled *display of God's love.* "God commendeth his love toward us, in that, while we were yet sinners, Christ died for us." Oh to think of it, that He who was offended takes the nature of the offender, and then bears the penalty due for wanton transgression. He who is infinite, thrice holy, all glorious, for ever to be worshipped, yet stoopeth to be numbered with the transgressors, and to bear the sin of many. The mythology of the gods of high Olympus contains nothing worthy to be mentioned in the same day with this wondrous deed of supreme condescension and infinite love. The ancient Shasters and Vedas have nothing of the kind. The death of Jesus Christ upon the cross cannot be an invention of men; none of the ages have produced aught like it in the poetic dreams of any nation. If we did not hear of it so often, and think of it so little, we should be charmed with it beyond expression.

I believe again, thirdly, that Paul delighted to preach the cross of Christ as *the removal of all guilt.* He believed that the Lord Jesus on the cross finished transgression, made an end of sin, and brought in everlasting righteousness. He that believeth in Jesus is justified from all things from which he could not be justified by the law of Moses. Since sin was laid on Jesus, God's justice cannot lay it upon the believing sinner. The Lord will never punish twice the same offence. If He accepts a substitute for me, how can He call me to His bar and punish me for that transgression, for which my substitute endured the chastisement? Many a troubled conscience has caught at this and found deliverance from despair. Wonder not that Paul gloried in Christ, since it is written, "In the Lord shall all the seed of Israel be justified, and shall glory." This is the method of salvation which completely and eternally absolves the sinner, and makes the blackest offender white as snow.

He glories in it, again, as *a marvel of wisdom*. It seemed to him the sum of perfect wisdom and skill. He cries, "O the depths of the riches both of the wisdom and knowledge of God!" The plan of salvation by vicarious suffering is simple, but sublime. It would have been impossible for human or angelic wisdom to have invented it. Men already so hate it and fight against it that they never would have advised it. God alone out of the treasury of His infinite wisdom brought forth this matchless project of salvation for the guilty through the substitution of the innocent. The more we study it, the more we shall perceive that it is full of teaching.

It is only the superficial thinker who regards the cross as a subject soon to be comprehended and exhausted: the most lofty intellects will here find ample room and verge enough. The profoundest minds might lose themselves in considering the splendid diversities of light which compose the pure white light of the cross. Everything of sin and justice, of misery and mercy, of folly and wisdom, of force and tenderness, or rage and pity, on the part of man and God, may be seen here. In the cross may be seen the concentration of eternal thought, the focus of infinite purpose, the outcome of illimitable wisdom. Of God and the cross we may say:

> "Here I behold His inmost heart,
>   Where grace and vengeance strangely join;
>   Piercing His Son with sharpest smart
>   To make the purchased pleasures mine."

I believe that Paul gloried in the cross, again, because it is *the door of hope*, even to the vilest of the vile. The world was very filthy in Paul's time. Roman civilization was of the most brutal and debased kind, and the masses of the people were sunken in vices that are altogether unmentionable. Paul felt that he could go into the darkest places with light in his hand when he spoke of the cross. To tell of pardon bought with the blood of the

Son of God is to carry an omnipotent message. The cross uplifts the fallen and delivers the despairing. The cross is the standard of victorious grace. It is the light-house whose cheering ray gleams across the dark waters of despair and cheers the dense midnight of our fallen race, saving from eternal shipwreck, and piloting into everlasting peace.

Again, Paul, I believe, gloried in the cross, as I often do, because it was *the source of rest* to him and to his brethren. I make this confession, and I make it very boldly, that I never knew what rest of heart truly meant till I understood the doctrine of the substitution of our Lord Jesus Christ. Now, when I see my Lord bearing away my sins as my scapegoat, or dying for them as my sin-offering, I feel a profound peace of heart and satisfaction of spirit. The cross is all I want for security and joy. Truly, this bed is long enough for a man to stretch himself on it. The cross is a chariot of salvation, wherein we traverse the high road of life without fear. The pillow of atonement heals the head that aches with anguish. Beneath the shadow of the cross I sit down with great delight, and its fruit is sweet unto my taste. I have no impatience even to haste to heaven while resting beneath the cross, for our hymn truly says:

> "Here it is I find my heaven,
>   While upon the cross I gaze."

Here is perfect cleansing, and hence a divine security, guarded by the justice of God; and hence a "peace of God, which passeth all understanding." To try to entice me away from the truth of substitution is labour in vain. Seduce me to preach the pretty nothings of modern thought! This child knows much better than to leave the substance for the shadow, the truth for the fancy. I see nothing that can give to my heart a fair exchange for the rest, peace, and unutterable joy which the old-fashioned doctrine of the cross now yields me. I cannot go beyond my simple faith that Jesus stood in my stead, and bore my sin, and put my sin away. This I must preach; I know nothing else. God helping me I will never go an inch beyond the cross, for to me all else is vanity and vexation of spirit. Return unto thy rest, O my soul! Where else is there a glimpse of hope for thee but in Him who loved thee and gave Himself for thee?

I am sure Paul gloried in the cross yet again because he saw it to be *the creator of enthusiasm.* Christianity finds its chief force in the enthusiasm which the Holy Ghost produces; and this comes from the cross. The preaching of the cross is the great weapon of the crusade against evil. A something lies within the truth of the cross which sets the soul aglow; it touches the preacher's lips as with a live coal, and fires the hearer's hearts as with flame from the altar of God. We can on this gospel live, and for this gospel die. Atonement by blood, full deliverance from sin, perfect safety in Christ given to the believer, call a man to joy, to gratitude, to consecration, to decision, to patience, to holy living, to all-consuming zeal. Therefore in the doctrine of the cross we glory, neither will we be slow to speak it out with all our might.

III. My time has gone, or else I had intended to have enlarged upon the third head, of which I must now give you the mere outline. One of Paul's great reasons for glorying in the cross was its action upon himself. WHAT WAS ITS EFFECT UPON HIM?

The cross is never without influence. Come where it may, it worketh for life or for death. "The world is crucified to me, and I unto the world." Self and the world are both crucified when Christ's cross appears and is believed in. Beloved, what does Paul mean? Does he not mean just this—that ever since he had seen Christ he looked upon the world as a crucified, hanged up, gibbeted thing, which had no charms for him, whose frown he did not fear, whose love he did not court. The world had no more power over Paul than a criminal hanged upon a cross. What power has a corpse on a gibbet? Such power had the world over Paul. The world despised him, and he could not go after the world if he would, and would not go after it if he could. He was dead to it, and it was dead to him: thus there was a double separation.

How does the cross do this? To be under the dominion of this present evil world is horrible; how does the cross help us to escape? Why, brethren, he that has ever seen the cross looks upon the world's pomp and glory as a vain show. The pride of heraldry and the glitter of honour fade into meanness before the Crucified One. O ye great ones, what are your silks, and your furs, and your jewellery, and your gold, your stars and your garters, to one who has learned to glory in Christ crucified! The old clothes which belong to the hangman are quite as precious. The world's light is darkness when the Sun of Righteousness shines from the tree. What care we for all the kingdoms of the world and the glory thereof when once we see the thorn-crowned Lord? There is more glory about one nail of the cross than about all the sceptres of all kings. Let the knights of the Golden Fleece meet in chapter, and all the Knights of the Garter stand in their stalls, and what is all their splendour? Their glories wither before the inevitable hour of doom, while the glory of the cross is eternal. Everything of earth grows dull and dim when seen by cross light.

Paul also saw that the world's *wisdom* was absurd. That age talked of being wise and philosophical! Yes, and its philosophy

brought it to crucify the Lord of glory. It did not know perfection, nor perceive the beauty of pure unselfishness. To slay
the Messiah was the outcome of the culture of the Pharisee,
to put to death the greatest teacher of all time was the ripe fruit
of Sadducean thought. The cogitations of the present age have
performed no greater feat than to deny the doctrine of satisfaction
for sin. They have crucified our Lord afresh by their criticisms
and their new theologies; and this is all the world's wisdom ever
does. Its wisdom lies in scattering doubt, quenching hope, and
denying certainty; and therefore the wisdom of the world to us
is sheer folly. God hath poured contempt upon the wise men of
this world; their foolish heart is blinded, they grope at noonday.

So, too, the apostle saw the world's *religion* to be nought. It
was the world's religion that crucified Christ, the priests were at
the bottom of it, the Pharisees urged it on. The church of the
nation, the church of many ceremonies, the church which loved
the traditions of the elders, the church of phylacteries and broad-
bordered garments—it was this church, which, acting by its
officers, crucified the Lord. Paul therefore looked with pity
upon priests and altars, and upon all the attempts of a Christless
world to make up by finery of worship for the absence of the
Spirit of God. Once see Christ on the cross, and architecture
and fine display become meretricious, tawdry things. The
cross calls for worship in spirit and in truth, and the world knows
nothing of this.

And so it was with the world's *pursuits*. Some ran after honour,
some toiled after learning, others laboured for riches; but to
Paul these were all trifles since he had seen Christ on the cross.
He that has seen Jesus die will never go into the toy business;
he puts away childish things. A child, a pipe, a little soap, and
many pretty bubbles: such is the world. The cross alone can
wean us from such play.

And so it was with the world's *pleasures* and with the world's
power. The world, and everything that belonged to the world,
had become as a corpse to Paul, and he was as a corpse to it.
See where the corpse swings in chains on the gibbet. What a
foul, rotten thing! We cannot endure it! Do not let it hang
longer above ground to fill the air with pestilence. Let the dead
be buried out of sight. The Christ that died upon the cross now
lives in our hearts. The Christ that took human guilt has taken
possession of our souls, and henceforth we live only in Him, for
Him, by Him. He has engrossed our affections. All our
ardours burn for Him. God make it to be so with us, that we
may glorify God and bless our age.

Paul concludes this epistle by saying, "From henceforth let
no man trouble me: for I bear in my body the marks of the Lord

Jesus.'' He was a slave, branded with his Master's name. That stamp could never be got out, for it was burned into his heart. Even thus, I trust, the doctrine of the atonement is our settled belief, and faith in it is part of our life. We are rooted and grounded in the unchanging verities. Do not try to convert me to your new views; I am past it. Give me over. You waste your breath. It is done: on this point the wax takes no further impress. I have taken up my standing, and will never quit it. A crucified Christ has taken such possession of my entire nature, spirit, soul, and body, that I am henceforth beyond the reach of opposing arguments.

Brethren, sisters, will you enlist under the conquering banner of the cross? Once rolled in the dust and stained in blood, it now leads on the armies of the Lord to victory! Oh that all ministers would preach the true doctrine of the cross! Oh that all Christian people would live under the influence of it, and we should then see brighter days than these! Unto the Crucified be glory for ever and ever. Amen.